GRAMMAR OF THE KASHMIRI LANGUAGE

A GRAMMAR OF THE KASHMIRI LANGUAGE

AS SPOKEN IN THE VALLEY OF KASHMIR

T. R. WADE

WITH AN INTRODUCTION BY
ROBERT CUST

GYAN

Published by

Gyan Publishing House
5, Ansari Road
Daryaganj, New Delhi-110002
Phone: 011-47034999, 9811692060
E-mail: books@gyanbooks.com

Distribution Network
gyanbooks.com
India, USA, Canada, UK, Australia, France

ISBN : 978-81-212-4391-9 (PB)
First Published, London, 1888

2nd Impression 2020

Printed at: Gyan Press, Delhi.

A Grammar of the Kashmiri Language
Author: T. R. Wade

A GRAMMAR

OF THE

KASHMĪRĪ LANGUAGE.

A GRAMMAR

OF THE

KASHMĪRĪ LANGUAGE,

AS SPOKEN IN THE

VALLEY OF KASHMĪR, NORTH INDIA.

BY THE

REV. T. R. WADE, B.D., M.R.A.S.,

OF THE CHURCH MISSIONARY SOCIETY.

WITH AN INTRODUCTION BY

DR. ROBERT CUST.

LONDON:

SOCIETY FOR PROMOTING CHRISTIAN KNOWLEDGE,

NORTHUMBERLAND AVENUE, CHARING CROSS, W.C.

1888.

PREFACE.

THE following pages have been compiled from notes which I made whilst labouring as a missionary of the Church Missionary Society for some years in Kashmīr; and they are now published in the hope that, however imperfect, they may be of some use to the present and future missionaries in the country of Kashmīr, and to the many tourists who yearly visit it, and also that they may possibly serve as some help towards a better, larger, and more critical grammar of the language.

The Vale of Kashmīr, or Kashmīr Proper, situated to the north of the Punjāb, is of an irregular oval shape, elevated a little over five thousand feet above the sea-level, generally sloping from south-east to north-west, about eighty miles long, and from twenty to twenty-five broad, containing an area of something less than two thousand square miles. It is entirely surrounded by mountains, which rise, on the north-east side, to about eighteen thousand feet. In latitude, Kashmīr corresponds nearly with Peshāwar, Bāghdād, and Damascus, in Asia; with Fez, in Morocco, in Africa; and with South Carolina, in America; but, on account of its situation and altitude, it possesses a climate which can compare most favourably with any of these. Speaking generally, I should say it is a little colder in winter and a little hotter in summer, but otherwise much like the climate of England, and very healthy.*

The people are, in size and in feature, one of the finest races on the whole continent of India, and are capable of the highest mental training. The face of the Kashmīrī, especially of the Kashmīrī Brahman, is of the pure High-Ayran type; the peasantry are generally good-looking, robust, and of great muscular power.

The population of Kashmīr, according to the census of the Jummoo and Kashmīr territories for 1873, was—Hindus, 61,132; Muhammadāns, 427,488; sundry castes, 3226; total, 491,846.

The Kashmīrī language is a descendant of one of the ancient Prākrit dialects. As might be expected from a knowledge of the history of the country, modern Kashmīrī has imported a large number of Persian and Arabic words; some have been borrowed from the Tibeto-Burman and Altaic languages on the north and north-east, and an ever-increasing number of words are now being introduced from Punjābī and Hindustānī. I have given some idea of the number of these words in Kashmīrī at page 109 of this Grammar.

* "As regards vegetation and climate, it (Kashmīr) somewhat resembles the mildest parts of the south of England" ("Lahore to Yarkand," p. 33, by Dr. G. Henderson and A. O. Hume, Esq.). Speaking of the mountains of Kashmīr, Dr. Henderson says, "I have seen a man walking regularly his thirty miles a day over difficult ground, who, on starting, two months before, had to ride, or get carried, two-thirds of every march. The remarkable thing is that even a person of delicate health does not suffer from the exposure, and one never by any chance catches a cold, at least in the mountains beyond Kashmīr, where the climate is exceedingly dry" (page 35).

There being several dialects spoken in the valley, and the vast majority of the people being entirely uneducated, it will be easily understood how difficult was the work of compiling this Grammar. Different persons would pronounce the same word differently, and would not spell it always in the same way, and there was no written authority to which to appeal.

The Muhammadāns, who form a very large majority of the population of Kashmīr, use many more Persian and Arabic words than the Hindus; and an increasing number of those who live in the large cities—the merchants and traders and others, who come most in contact with visitors and their servants—can speak Hindustānī; and some few can make themselves understood in English. There is at present a great desire on the part of many young men, pundits especially, in Srinagar to acquire English, and some of them have made considerable progress in learning it. The Brahman Hindus, and the *Jōtish* Hindus, who are engaged in various offices of their religion, use very few Persian and Arabic words, and so with their wives and families; whilst many of the *Kārkun* Hindus, especially those who are writers, are well able to speak and write Persian. Indeed, the court language of Kashmīr for several centuries, under the Moghuls, the Pathāns, and even the Sikhs, has been and is Persian.

Kāshmīrī is closely allied to the Pahāri, or hill dialects, spoken in the districts bordering on Kashmīr; as Kishtwārī, Pādarī, Bhadarwātrī, Rāmbanī, etc.; and through these a connection can be easily traced with Dogrī, Punjābī, and Hindustānī.

The proverbs in this Grammar have been taken from a collection I myself made when residing in Kashmīr, and also from the "Dictionary of Kashmīrī Proverbs and Sayings," by the Rev. J. Hinton Knowles.

As I have carried this work through the press whilst in England, and was therefore unable to get assistance from any pandit or munshī who knew Kashmīrī, and had other and pressing engagements on hand at the same time, I must crave the considerate indulgence of the student for any mistakes which he may find.

T. RUSSELL WADE.

BELMONT PARK, LEE,
September, 1888.

INTRODUCTION.

THE Kashmiri is a separate and distinct language of the Indic branch of the great Indo-European or Aryan family of languages, which extends from India to the Atlantic Ocean. It is alluded to by name by Marco Paolo and Ab-ul-Fazal. The term "Kashmīrī," as a language, is held to include several dialects spoken in the adjacent hills, but their variations in phonetics, structure, and word-store, have not yet been scientifically analyzed. There is a special written character, akin to though distinct from the Nāgari.

A Grammar and proper Texts have long been linguistic desiderata. In my "Modern Languages of the East Indies" (Trübner: 1878) I drew attention to this fact, and it is to me a great satisfaction that the Rev. T. R. Wade, a missionary of the Church Missionary Society, during his official residence in the valley, has found leisure to compile the Grammar to which this is an Introduction. Mr. Wade has also supplied Texts in the form of translations of the Holy Scriptures. I commend this volume to the favourable notice of all Aryan scholars.

ROBERT CUST,

Honorary Secretary of the Royal Asiatic Society and Member of the Translation Committee of the Society for Promoting Christian Knowledge.

LONDON,
September, 1888.

CONTENTS.

THE DEVANĀGARI AND SHĀRADA ALPHABETS.

Vowels.

Devanāgari.	Shārada.	English.	Devanāgari.	Shārada.	English.
अ	𑆃	a	अक्ताभ	𑆃𑆑𑆠𑆳𑆨	aktābh, *sun.*
आ	𑆄	ā	आनन्द	𑆄𑆤𑆤𑇀𑆢	Ānand, *Anand.* [Proper name.]
इ	𑆅	i	इम्भरी	𑆅𑆩𑇀𑆨𑆫𑆵	Imbhari, *Imbhari.* [Proper name.]
ई	𑆆	ī	ईश्वरा	𑆆𑆯𑇀𑆮𑆫𑆳	Īshvarā, *God.*
उ	𑆇	u	उर्दू	𑆇𑆫𑇀𑆢𑆷	Urdu, *Urdu.*
ऊ	𑆈	ū	ऊंगान	𑆈𑆁𑆓𑆳𑆤	ūngān, *cry of fox.*
ऋ	𑆉	ri	ऋरथ	𑆉𑆡	reth, *month.*
ए	𑆍	e	एक	𑆍𑆑	ek, *one.*
ऐ	𑆎	ai	ऐसा	𑆎𑆱𑆳	aisa, *so.*
ओ	𑆏	o	ओन	𑆏𑆤	on, *blind.*
औ	𑆐	au	औशाद	𑆐𑆯𑆳𑆢	Aushād, *Aushad.* [Proper name.]

Consonants.

Devanāgari.	Shārada.	English.	Devanāgari.	Shārada.	English.
क	𑆑	k	करीमा	𑆑𑆫𑆵𑆩𑆳	Karīmā, *Karima.* [Proper name.]
ख	𑆒	kh	खर	𑆒𑆫	khār, *donkey.*
ग	𑆓	g	गुनस	𑆓𑆶𑆤𑆱	gunas, *snake.*
घ	𑆔	gh	घ्रटु	𑆔𑇀𑆫𑆛𑆶	ghraṭ[u], *millstone.*
ङ	𑆕	n	कङं	𑆑𑆕	kans {*hollow of a mortar for pounding rice.*
च	𑆖	ch (*ts*)	चाश्चाठ	𑆖𑆳𑆯𑇀𑆖𑆳𑆜	(ch)tsath, *disciple.*
छ	𑆗	chh	छान	𑆗𑆳𑆤	chhān, *carpenter.*
ज	𑆘	j	जान	𑆘𑆳𑆤	jān, *well.*
झ	𑆙	jh	झन	𑆙𑆤	jhan, *world.*
ञ	𑆚	n	ञारुन	𑆚𑆳𑆫𑆶𑆤	Nārun, *Nārun.* [Proper name.]

CONSONANTS—*continued.*

DEVANĀGARI.	SHĀRADA.	ENGLISH.	DEVANĀGARI.	SHĀRADA.	ENGLISH.
ट	𑆛	ṭ	टास	𑆛𑆳𑆱	ṭās, *sound.*
ठ	𑆜	ṭh	ठाकुर	𑆜𑆳𑆑𑆶𑆫	ṭhākur, *idol.*
ड	𑆝	ḍ	डमडम	𑆝𑆩𑆝𑆩	ḍamḍam, *drum.*
ढ	𑆞	ḍh	ढांग	𑆞𑆳𑆁𑆓	ḍhāng, *stick.*
ण	𑆟	ṇ	अणुद	𑆄𑆟𑆶𑆢	aṇud, *cook.*
त	𑆠	t	तोत	𑆠𑆾𑆠	tota, *parrot.*
थ	𑆡	th	थम	𑆡𑆩	tham, *prop.*
द	𑆢	d	दमह	𑆢𑆩𑆲	damah, *name of a sickness.*
ध	𑆣	dh	धर्म	𑆣𑆫𑇀𑆩	dharm, *gift, good work.*
न	𑆤	n	नाग	𑆤𑆳𑆓	nāg, *serpent.*
प	𑆥	p	पंपुश	𑆥𑆁𑆥𑆾𑆯	pamposh, *water lily*
फ	𑆦	ph	फिरन	𑆦𑆴𑆫𑆤	phéran, *garment.*
ब	𑆧	b	बतिज़	𑆧𑆠𑆴𑆘	batij, *duck.*
भ	𑆨	bh	भता	𑆨𑆠𑆳	bhata, *food.*
म	𑆩	m	महोल	𑆩𑆲𑆾𑆬	mahol, *pestle.*
य	𑆪	y	यार	𑆪𑆳𑆫	yār, *friend.*
र	𑆫	r	रस	𑆫𑆱	ras, *juice.*
ल	𑆬	l	लार	𑆬𑆳𑆫	Lār, *Lār.* [Name of district.]
व	𑆮	w, v	वान	𑆮𑆳𑆤	wān, *wood.*
श	𑆯	ś, sh	शाल	𑆯𑆳𑆬	shāl, *jackal.*
ष	𑆰	sh	षाभान	𑆰𑆳𑆨𑆳𑆤	Shābhān, *Shabhan.* [Name of month.]
स	𑆱	s	सुल्तान	𑆱𑆶𑆬𑆠𑆳𑆤	sultān, *sultān.*
ह	𑆲	h	हापुत	𑆲𑆳𑆥𑆶𑆠	hāput, *bear.*

KASHMĪRĪ GRAMMAR.

CHAPTER I.

LETTERS.

1. Kashmīrī is written in the Dewanāgari, Shārada (a modified form of Dewanāgari), and Persian characters. In writing the language in the Roman characters, the ordinary Roman-Urdu system will be followed, with some few additional vowels to represent sounds peculiar to Kashmīrī.

The Alphabet.

1. *Consonants.*

Letters.		Pronunciation.	Examples.
'	'	Arabic ع, a peculiar guttural sound	Represented by an ' before its vowel; as, 'aql, *wisdom;* 'ilm, *science;* 'umr, *age*
B	b	As in English	Bar, *a door*
Ch	ch	Persian چ, as in "church"	Chôbur, *young*
D	d	Sanskrit द, more dental than the English *d*	Dod, *pain*

Letters.		Pronunciation.	Examples.
Ḍ	ḍ	Sanskrit ड, tongue well turned up towards roof of mouth when pronouncing it	Ḍoṛa, *a rope*
F	f	As in English	Farsh, *a carpet*
G	g	As in English (always hard)	Gagur, *a rat*
G͟h	g͟h	Arabic غ, a strong guttural	G͟husal, *a bath*
H	h	As in English	Hôst, *an elephant*
Ḥ	ḥ	Arabic ح, a strong aspirate, uttered by compressing lower muscles of throat	Raḥīm, *merciful*
J	j	As in English	Jān, *good*
K	k	As in English	Kul, *a tree*
K͟h	k͟h	Arabic خ, a strong guttural	K͟hudā, *God*
L	l	As in English	Laṛ, *a house*
M	m	As in English	Mol, *father*
N	n	As in English	Nun, *salt*
Ṇ	ṇ	*n* nasal	Ṇiām, *mortar*
P	p	As in English	Posh, *a flower*
Q	q	Arabic ق, pronounced from lower muscles of throat	Banduq, *a gun*
R	r	Pronounced very distinctly	Run, *husband*
Ṛ	ṛ	Urdu ڑ, the tip of tongue turned well up towards roof of mouth	Muṛ, *myrrh*
S	s	As in English	Sôn, *gold*
Ṣ	ṣ	Arabic ص, much like English *sw*	Qaṣd, *intention*

Letters.		Pronunciation.	Examples.
S̤	s̤	Arabic ث, much like English *s*, with a little of *th* in it	S̤awạb, *future reward of virtue*
Sh	sh	Arabic ش, as in English	Shur, *a child*
T	t	Sanskrit त, very soft and dental	Tot, *beloved*
Ṭ	ṭ	Sanskrit ट, tongue well turned up towards roof of mouth	Ṭhokar, *a blow*
T̲s̲	t̲s̲	Sanskrit च, *ch*, but pronounced *t̲s̲* in Kashmīrī	T̲s̲ur, *a thief*
T̤	t̤	Arabic ط, harsher than *t*	K̲h̲at̤, *a letter*
V	v	As in English	Vīr, *a willow*
W	w	A little more of the sound of the *v* in it than in English	Wonun, *to weave*
Y	y	As in English	Yār, *a friend*
Z	z	As in English	Zun, *the moon*
Ẓ	ẓ	Arabic ض, a mixture of *d*, *th*, and *w*	K̲h̲iẓar, *name of a man*
Z̤	z̤	Arabic ظ, much like *tz*	Ḥifz̤, *memory*
Z̲	z̲	Arabic ذ, much as *z*	Kāg̲h̲az̲, *paper*
Z̲h̲	z̲h̲	Persian ژ, like *z* in "azure"	Paz̲h̲murda, *faded*

2. Of the above letters, *Ḥ*, *Q*, *S̤*, *Ṣ*, *T̤*, *Ẓ*, *Z̤*, ', are peculiar to Arabic; *Z̲h̲*, to Persian; *T̲s̲*, to Kashmīrī; *G̲h̲*, *K̲h̲*, *Z*, *Z̲*, to Arabic and Persian; *Ṭ*, *Ḍ*, *Ṛ*, are Indian; *P*, *C̲h̲*, and *G*, are Persian and Indian, but not Arabic; and the remaining letters are common. Consequently, words containing any of the letters peculiar to Arabic must be from that language;

words having *Zh* must be of Persian origin; those having *Ts* must be Kashmīrī; those with *Gh*, *Kh*, *Z*, *Z̤*, may be Arabic or Persian; those with *P*, *Ch*, *G*, may be Persian or Indian; and words having any of the letters *Ṭ*, *Ḍ*, *Ṛ*, in them are of Indian origin.

3. Of the thirteen letters peculiar to Arabic and Persian only one of them, *Z*, receives its particular pronunciation from the uneducated people in Kashmīr. *Gh* is pronounced as *G*; *Ḥ*, as *H*; *Kh*, as *K*; *Ṣ*, *S̤*, as *S*; *Ṭ*, as *T*; and *Ẓ*, *Z̤*, *Z*, *Zh*, as *Z*.

Those who have studied Persian or Arabic are more particular in their pronunciation, and in writing these languages the words are properly spelt. Also when Kashmīrī is written in the Persian character, Persian and Arabic words are written correctly, and not as they are pronounced by the common people. The word for "God," for instance, in Persian is *Khudā*, but generally pronounced by the ordinary Kashmīrī *Kudā*, yet always written in the Persian character, خدا, *Khudā*.

2. *Vowels.*

Letters.		Pronunciation.	Examples.
A	a	Short *a*, as in "woman," "adrift"	Bar, *a door*
Ā	ā	Long *a*, as in "war," "father"	Ār, *mercy*
Ạ	ạ	Peculiar; a short *a* sound from the throat	Zạṭh, *a rag*
E	e	Long *e*, as *ea* in "bear" or *ai* in "fail"	Her, *a ladder*
Ė	ė	Short *e*, as in "met," "bet," "let"	Mėts, *earth*
I	i	Short *i*, as in "mill," "bill"	Hil, *water-grass*
Ī	ī	Long *i*, as in "machine," "police"	Mīl, *ink*

LETTERS.	PRONUNCIATION.	EXAMPLES.
O o	Long *o*, as in "hole," "mole"	Mol, *father*
Ȯ ȯ	Short *o*, as in "cot," "hot"	Vȯdur, *an otter*
Ö ö	Peculiar; much like the German *ö*	Dör, *beard*
U u	Short *u*, as in "pull," "bull"	Gur, *a horse*
Ū ū	Long *u*, as in "rule," "rude"	Kūr, *a daughter*
Ū̃ ū̃	Peculiar; a long *ạ* sound from the throat	Tū̃r, *cold*

4. Of the above vowels, *ā*, *a*, *e*, *ī*, *i*, *o*, *ū*, *u*, are the same as those used in writing Hindustānī in Roman characters, whilst *ạ*, *ė*, *ȯ*, *ö*, *ū̃*, are peculiar to Kashmīrī. In some few Roman-Urdu books *ạ* is used to represent the ع with a fatḥa; but this will not make a great difficulty, as the Kashmīrī *ạ* is a short *a* sound from the throat, though not so guttural as the Arabic ع.

The vowels, as given by Dr. Forbes in his "Hindustānī Grammar," are—

English words: fall, fun, fail, feel, fin, foal, fool, foot.

Roman-Urdu: fāl, fan, fel, fīl, fin, fol, fūl, fut.

The letters *ė* and *ȯ* are simply the short sounds of these letters, as in "pet," "met," "not," "rot." The *ö* is almost identical with the German *ö*, but the *ạ* and the *ū̃* can only be learned from a native, as there are no sounds like them in the English language. The *ạ* sound is very common,—it occurs in almost every sentence; whilst there are not many words that have the peculiar *ū̃* sound.

5. The diphthongs *ai* and *au* will have the same sounds as in Roman-Urdu.

6. There are also two very short vowel-sounds in the

language: A half *u* sound at the end of some words, particularly those of the second declension of nouns. As this is almost imperceptible and difficult to represent, I omit it in this work. The other is a very short *i* sound, which will be represented by a small *ị* in italics with a dot under it. It must be understood that this is much shorter than the short *i*, and is only just perceptible; still it is important; for instance, *gur*, or more correctly, *gur^u*, is "a horse," *$gur^ị$*, horses.

CHAPTER II.

NOUNS.

7. There are four declensions in Kashmīrī; and generally nouns of the first two declensions are masculine, and those of the other two feminine. Nouns may be thus declined—

I. Declension.

Case.	Singular.	Plural.
Nominative and *Accusative*	tsur, *a thief*	tsur, *thieves*
Genitive	tsura sund,* etc., *of a thief*	tsuran hund,* etc., *of thieves*
Dative	tsuras, *to a thief*	tsuran, *to thieves*
Agentive	tsuran, *by a thief*	tsurau, *by thieves*
Locative	tsuras nish, *near a thief*	tsuran nish, *near thieves*
Ablative	tsuras nishi, *from a thief* gara andarạ, *from a house*	tsurau nishi, *from thieves*
Vocative	hatā, etc., tsurā, / hatā, etc., tsuro, *O thief*	hatā, etc., tsurau, *O thieves*

* *Sund* and *hund* are inflected to agree with the objects possessed in gender and number (*vide* pars. 22, 23).

8. When a noun of this declension ends in a vowel, *h* is added before the terminations *-as*, *-an*, etc.; as, *sazā*, punishment, *sazāhas*, *sazāhan*; *Musā*, Moses, *Musāhas*, etc.

9. By adding *ā* to a noun, the meaning becomes indefinite, as *tsurā*, any thief; by adding *ại*, the noun is rendered definite, as *tsurại*, that particular thief: *ại* here in Kashmīrī answers to *hī* in Hindustānī.

10. Examples of nouns of this declension: *Nār*, fire; *bar*, a door; *dānd*, an ox; *kalam*, a pen; *āb*, water; *kōkạr*, a fowl; *bata*, or *bhata*, food; *garạ*, a house; *hāk*, vegetable; *goguj*, a turnip, *gogajas*; *gāzar*, a carrot; *mez*, a table.

II. Declension.

Case.	Singular.	Plural.
Nom. / *Acc.*	gur, *a horse*	gur^i, *horses*
Gen.	gurị sund, etc., *of a horse*	gur^{i}ên hund, etc., *of horses*
Dat.	guris, *to a horse*	gur^{i}ên, *to horses*
Ag.	gur^i, *by a horse*	gur^{i}au, *by horses*
Loc.	guris nish, *near a horse*	gur^{i}ên nish, *near horses*
Ab.	guris nishi, *from a horse*	guriau andarạ, *from horses*
Voc.	hatā, etc., gur^{i}ā, / hatā, etc., gur^{i}o, } *O horse*	hatā, etc., gur^{i}au, *O horses*

11. Nouns of this declension, in the nominative and accusative singular, have an almost imperceptible *u* sound after them; thus, *gur*^{u}, a horse.

12. The vowel *o* of nouns of this declension is changed in the plural and in the inflected forms into *ö* or *ā*; as, *boi*, a brother, plu. *böi*, dat. sing. *böyis*; *tsong*, a lamp, plu. *tsāngị*, dat. sing. *tsāngis*; *khoṇkh*, one who speaks through his nose,

plu. *khönkhi*, dat. sing. *khönkhis.* *U* is sometimes changed into *ȯ*, *ö*, or *ạ*; as, *hun*, a dog, *hȯnis*; *krur*, a well, *kröris*; *hāput*, a bear, *hāpạtis.*

13. Examples of nouns of this declension: *Hȯst*, an elephant; *shur*, a ċhild; *kul*, a tree; *kȯb*, a hunchback; *ponz*, a monkey; *wagaw*, *wagawis*, matting; *satarand*, a durrie (kind of carpet), *sataranjis*; *khar*, an ass; *saraf*, a snake.

III. Declension.

Case.	Singular.	Plural.
Nom. } *Acc.* }	möj, *a mother*	māji, mājih, *mothers*
Gen.	māji hund, etc., *of a mother*	mājiēn hund, etc., *of mothers*
Dat.	māji, mājih, *to a mother*	mājiēn, *to mothers*
Ag.	māji, mājih, *by a mother*	mājiau, *by mothers*
Loc.	māji nish, *near a mother*	mājiēn nish, *near mothers*
Ab.	māji nishi, *from a mother*	mājiau andarạ, *from mothers*
Voc.	{hatāi, etc., möj, / hatā, etc., möjöi,} *O mother*	hatāi, etc., mājiau, *O mothers*

14. The vowel *ö* of nouns of this declension is always changed into *ā* in the plural and in the inflected forms; as, *dör*, a beard, plu. *dāri*; *kör*, the neck, *kāri*; *yör*, a fir tree, *yāri*: *ū* often into *o*; as, *kūr*, a daughter, *kori*; *lūr*, a stick, *lori*: and *ạ* into *a*; as, *gạb*, a sheep, *gabi*: though in polysyllabic words the *ạ* remains; as, *babạr*, a flower, *babạri*; *dadạr*, a cucumber, *dadạri*; *devi*, a goddess, in the inflect. plu. makes *deviyau*; *zạṭ*, a rag, makes plu. *zachi.*

15. When emphasis is required, an *h* is always added to the forms ending in *i*; as, "To whom did you give this?" Answer, *Mājih*, "To *mother*."

16. Examples of nouns of this declension: *Vör*, a small pot; *tör*, lateness; *köm*, work; *hètạr*, leprosy; *vöj*, a ring; *hör*, a bird (the *Mainā-Coracias Indica*); *zun*, the moon; *buṇ*, the chinār tree (*Platanus Orientalis*), *boṇi*; *zur*, a lampstand, *zuri*; *thūr*, an adze, *thori*.

IV. Declension.

Case.	Singular.	Plural.
Nom. *Acc.*	kitāb, *a book*	kitābạ, *books*
Gen.	kitạbi hund, etc., *of a book*	kitāban hund, etc., *of books*
Dat.	kitābi, kitābih, *to a book*	kitāban, *to books*
Ag.	kitābi, kitābih, *by a book*	kitābau, *by books*
Loc.	kitābi manz, *in a book*	kitāban manz, *in books*
Ab.	kitābi andarạ, *from a book*	kitābau andarạ, *from books*
Voc.	hatāi, etc., kitāb, *O book*	hatāi, etc., kitābau, *O books*

17. The vowel *ö* of nouns of this declension is changed into *ā*; as, *göḍ*, a fish, *gāḍi*, *gāḍan*.

18. Examples of nouns of this declension: *Süm*, a small bridge; *nazạr*, sight; *salām*, peace, salutation; *gunas*, a small snake found in Kashmīr.

19. Some nouns ending in *t* differ from the above example by adding *s* to the inflected forms and plural. *Rāt*, night, is thus declined—

Case.	Singular.	Plural.
Nom. / *Acc.*	rāt, *night*	röts, *nights*
Gen.	röts hund, etc., *of night*	rötsan hund, etc., *of nights*
Dat.	röts, *to night*	rötsan, *to nights*
Ag.	röts, *by night*	rötsau, *by nights*
Voc.	hatāi, etc., rāt, *O night*	hatāi, etc., rötsau, *O nights*

20. Vowel-changes. The vowel *ā* of monosyllabic nouns is changed into *ö*; as, *rāt*, *röts*. The *a* is changed into *ạ*; as, *ni'mat*, favour, plu. *ni'mạts*; *haqīqat*, truth, plu. *haqīqạts*.

Of Case.

21. The *Nominative* and *Accusative* cases are always the same. They are the nouns without any distinguishing signs.

22. The *Genitive* case may be expressed in four different ways: (1) by adding *sund* or *hund*, etc.; (2) by adding *uk*, etc.; (3) by adding *un*, etc.; (4) by adding *uv*, etc. *Sund*, with its inflections, is used with nouns of the first and second declensions in the singular; *hund*, with its inflections, is joined to plural nouns only of the first and second declensions, and to singular and plural nouns of the third and fourth declensions; *uk*, with its inflections, is only used with inanimate nouns of the first and second declensions; *un*, with its inflections, only with proper names; and *uv* denotes "made of." Each of the forms *sund*, *hund*, *uk*, *un*, and *uv*, always agrees with the object possessed in number and gender.

23. They are thus declined—

Singular.		Plural.	
Masculine.	Feminine.	Masculine.	Feminine.
sund	sạnz	sạnd^{i}	sạnzạ
hund	hạnz	hạnd^{i}	hạnzạ
uk	ạch	ạk^{i}	ạchi
un	ạn	ạn^{i}	ạni
uv	ạv	ạv^{i}	ạvi

24. Examples—

Nechavis sund mol, the son's father.
Nechavis sanz möj, the son's mother.
Nechavis sạndị gur^{i}, the son's horses.
Nechavis sạnzạ guri, the son's mares.
Māji hund k͟hāwind, the mother's husband.
Māji hạnz kūr, the mother's daughter.
Māji hạnd^{i} böi, the mother's brothers.
Māji hạnzạ kori, the mother's daughters.
Garuk mālik, the master of the house.
Garạch malikin, the mistress of the house.
Garạk^{i} t͟sāng^{i}, the lamps of the house.
Garạchi kitābạ, the books of the house.
Rām Chandun garạ, the house of Rām Chand.
Rām Chandạn kitāb, the book of Rām Chand.
Rām Chandạn^{i} gur^{i}, the horses of Rām Chand.
Rām Chandạni kori, the daughters of Rām Chand.
Hachuv garạ, a house of wood, a wooden house.
Hachạv lūr, a staff of wood, a wooden staff.
Hachạv^{i} krāv^{i}, sandals of wood, wooden sandals.
Hachavi dāri, windows of wood, wooden windows.

25. The *Dative* and *Locative* cases in each declension

have generally their singulars alike, and also their plurals; the locative is distinguished from the dative by its preposition.

26. The *Ablative* case is always known by its governing preposition; it is mostly like the dative in the singular number, and the agentive in the plural.

27. The *Agentive* case. In the first declension the agentive case singular is the same as the dative plural; in the second and third declensions the agentive singular is the same as the plural. It is the same also in the fourth declension with those nouns which follow the declension of *rāt*, but not with the others—those that follow the declension of *kitāb*.

For further particulars on the cases of nouns, see Syntax, chapter ix.

The Gender of Nouns.

28. All nouns are either masculine or feminine. The gender of a noun is generally determined either by its signification or its form.

Those nouns relating to males are masculine; as, *Rāma*, Rāma (proper name of a man); *Shankar*, Shankar; *bādshāh*, king; *k͟hāwind*, husband; *nechu*, son, boy. Those relating to females are feminine; as, *Fazli*, Fazli (proper name of a woman); *rāni*, wife of a rājā; *kolai*, wife; *āshēṇ*, wife; *bēni*, daughter.

29. The feminine is formed from the masculine by (1) a change of the last vowel, with sometimes a change also of the last consonant; (2) by adding certain affixes to the masculine noun.

(1) The following are the principal vowel-changes:—

	Masculine	Feminine
ā, o become ö	krāl, *a potter*	kröj, *a female potter*
	shāl, *a jackal*	shöj, *a female jackal*
	mol, *father*	möj, *mother*
	bror, *a tom-cat*	brör, *a female cat*
a, u̇, ȯ become ạ	kh̲ar, *an ass*	khạr *or* khạrin, *a female ass*
	gagu̇r, *a rat*	gagạr, *a female rat*
	zȯr, *a deaf man*	zạr, *a deaf woman*
	pȯt, *a plank*	pạt, *a small plank*

Examples of changes of consonants: *Vol* masc., a ring, *vöz* fem., a small ring for the finger; *wātul*, watul, a man of a low caste, *wātạj*, a female of the same caste; *batuk*, a drake; *batạch*, a duck; *ṭang* masc., a pear, *ṭạnch* fem.

30. (2) The principal affixes are—

-*ị*; as, *gur*, a horse, *gurị*, a mare.*

-*en̲* or -*in̲*; as, *saruf* masc., a snake, *sarafėn̲* fem., sometimes pronounced *sarup* and *sarupin̲*; *hȯn̲z*, a boatman, *hān̲zėn̲*, a boatwoman; *hȯst* masc., an elephant, *hȯstėn̲* fem.; *mazur* masc., a coolie, *muzrėn̲* fem.

-*bāi*; as, *dosil* masc., a mason, *dosilbāi* fem.; *chhān* masc., a carpenter, *chhānbāi* or *chhānạbāi* fem.

-*önị*: this affix is applied only to persons, denoting class, nation, or religion; as, *Gujar* masc., *Gujarönị* fem.; *Musalmān* masc., *Musalmönị* fem.; *Paṭhān* masc., *Paṭhönị* fem.; *Pundit* masc., *Punditönị* fem.

31. The gender is also sometimes marked by adding the words *mol*, father, and *möj*, mother; or *nar*, male, and *māda*, female; as, *doda mol*, a foster-father, *doda möj*, a foster-mother; *kh̲āna mol*, a beloved son, *kh̲āna möj*, a beloved daughter; *nar kotur*, a cock-pigeon, *māda kotur*, a hen-pigeon.

* In Hindustānī the feminine of *larkā* is *larki*; of *dhobi*, *dhobin*; of *kumhār*, *kumhāran*, or *kumhārani*.

32. Many words are quite different in the masculine and feminine; as, *run*, a husband, *āshėn̲*, a wife; *nechu*, a son, *kūr*, a daughter; *dānd*, a bull, *gau*, a cow; *kat*, a ram, *gạb*, a ewe; *mahaniu*, a man, *zanānạ*, a woman; *boi*, a brother, *bėni*, a sister; *kān̤tur*, a cock-sparrow, *t̲sar*, a hen-sparrow.

33. When the same nouns are used in Hindustānī and Kashmīrī, they have generally the same gender; but there are some exceptions.

(1) Nouns that are *masculine* in Hindustānī and *feminine* in Kashmīrī: *köm*, work, pronounced *kom* by the pundits; *lashkar*, an army; *salām*, peace; *mahal*, palace.

(2) Nouns that are *feminine* in Hindustānī, but *masculine* in Kashmīrī: *'izzat*, honour; *dua'*, prayer; *madad*, help; *mez*, table; *sazā*, punishment; *shām*, evening; *mahabbat*, love; *t'arīf*, praise; *najāt*, salvation; *jān*, life; *ruh*, spirit; *poshāk*, clothing; *khurāk*, food; *jild*, book-cover; *bandūk*, gun; *dīwār*, wall; *'arz*, request; *gharaz*, object; *quwat*, strength; *dawā*, medicine.

Number of Nouns.

34. *Rule I.* Nouns of the first declension are often the same in the nominative plural as in the singular, though in nouns of more than one syllable there is frequently a change in the last vowel: *u* is changed into *a*; as, *gagur*, a rat, plu. *gagar*; *hāput*, a bear, plu. *hāpat*; but when the affix *-ur* denotes trade, or *wālā* in Hindustānī, then the *u* is changed into *ạ*; as, *kāndur*, a baker, plu. *kāndạr*; *rangur*, a dyer, plu. *rangạr*.

Examples of nouns that have the nominative singular and plural the same: *Ath*, hand; *ach*, eye; *kwar*, foot; *kan*, ear; *thar*, back; *dekh*, forehead; *yad*, belly; *khār*, a blacksmith; *mazur*, a labourer; *t̲sur*, a thief; *hön̤z*, a boatman; *sats*, a tailor; *dosil*, a mason; *chhān*, a carpenter.

35. *Rule II.* All nouns of the second declension which end in the very short ^{u} sound, form their plural by adding the ^{i}, and often with the change of a vowel (*vide* par. 29); as, *gur*, a horse, plu. *gur^i*; *mol*, father, plu. *möl^i*; but *boi*, brother, has plu. *böi*. Sometimes a vowel is omitted in the plural; as, *tiör*, a sheep, plu. *tir^i*; *tsion*, a pillar, plu. *tsiṇ^i*.

36. *Rule III.* Feminine nouns of the third and fourth declensions form their plurals generally by adding *i* and *ạ* respectively to the singulars, often with vowel-changes (*vide* par. 29); as, *gur^i*, a mare, plu. *guri*; *sum*, a small bridge, plu. *samạ*.

A few nouns of the fourth declension form their plural by adding *s*, with a change of the vowel; as, *rāt*, night, plu. *röts*; *ni'mat*, blessing, plu. *ni'mạts*.

CHAPTER III.

ADJECTIVES.

37. Adjectives in Kashmīrī are of two kinds—those that are declined to agree with their nouns in number, gender, and case; and those that are not declined.

38. The masculines of adjectives that are declined generally follow the second declension of nouns, and the feminines the third declension.

Example: *Wozul*, red, is thus declined—

Case.	Singular.		Plural.	
	Masculine.	Feminine.	Masculine.	Feminine.
Nom. *Acc.*	wozul	wozạj	wozạl^{i}	wozạji
Dat.	wozạlis	wozạji	wozạl^{i}ên	wozạj^{i}ên
Ag.	wozạl^{i}	wozạji	wozạl^{i}au	wozạj^{i}au
Loc.	wozạlis manz	wozạji manz	wozạl^{i}ên manz	wozạj^{i}ên
Ab.	wozạlis nishi	wozạji nishi	wozạl^{i}au andarạ	wozạj^{i}au
Voc.	wozạliā̃	wozạj	wozạl^{i}au	wozạj^{i}au

39. The feminine of adjectives is formed from the masculine according to the same rules as feminine nouns are formed from masculine nouns.

Examples: (i.) Changes of vowels—

o masc. becomes *ö* in fem., as	*toṭ*	masc.,	beloved,	*töṭ*	fem.
or, *ạ* ,, ,,	*moṭ*	,,	thick,	*mạṭ*	,,
ò ,, ,, *ạ* ,, ,,	*bòd*	,,	big,	*bạd*	,,
or, *ė* ,, ,,	*viòt*	,,	fat,	*viėt*	,,
	tiòt	,,	bitter,	*tiėt*	,,
u ,, ,, *ạ* ,, ,,	*kātsur*	,,	brown,	*kātsạr*	,,
or, *ū̃* ,, ,,	*kur*	,,	cruel,	*kū̃r*	,,
or, *ạ* ,, ,,	*wozul*	,,	red,	*wozạj*	,,
io ,, ,, *ī* ,, ,,	*miot*	,,	sweet,	*mīt* or *met*	,,

(ii.) Changes of consonants—

d masc. becomes *z* in fem., as	*thòd*	masc.,	high,	*thạz*	fem.
g ,, ,, *d* ,, ,,	*lòng*	,,	lame,	*land*	,,
k ,, ,, *ch* ,, ,,	*hòk*	,,	dry,	*hòch*	,,
t {in mono-syllables} *ts* ,, ,,	*sòt*	,,	slow,	*sạts*	,,
	mòt	,,	silly,	*mạts*	,,

40. The adjectives that are not declined are—

(1) Those that have *-lad* as an affix, denoting possession; as, *dod*, pain, *dödilad*, having pain, painful; *ālatslad*, idle; *krödạlad*, angry; *hètarilad*, having a disease of the skin.

(2) Adjectives from other languages; as, *sufed*, white, *sabz*, green; *bīmār*, ill; *kālā*, black.

(3) Adjectives ending in *ạ*; as, *budạ*, old; *bālạ*, young; *nākārạ*, worthless.

(4) The adjectives *jān*, good; *yachh*, bad; *mònd*, blunt; *sundar*, beautiful; *bewāi*, careless; *bèhwāl*, one who stays at home; *nèlradrāw*, one who frequently goes out.

41. Nouns or phrases in the inflected form are sometimes used with other nouns, and may then be regarded as adjectives, much as we say in English, "an iron safe," "a silk dress," "a glass cup," etc.; as, *hāri ṭang*, a cowrie pear, *i.e.* a pear that costs a cowrie; *muhari tsunṭ*, an apple that costs a muhr; *Hāpat yāraz*, Bear friendship (proverb); *gabi buthi rāmahun*, a sheep-faced wolf; *batak ṭhul*, a duck's egg.

42. *Kèṇtsa* is used to denote "rather" or "-ish" in English; as, *tsok*, sour; *kèṇtsa tsok*, rather sour, sourish.

43. The nouns *hana*, a piece, *hawāva*, a whiff or puff, and *moya*, little, are constantly used after inflected nouns to denote a little; as, *ābạ hawāva*, or *ābạ moya*, a little water, *bata hana*, a little food.

-han and *-hun* are also affixes to form diminutive nouns.

COMPARISON OF ADJECTIVES.

44. There are no inflections in Kashmīrī or regular suffixes added to adjectives to denote the degrees of comparison. The most common way of forming comparisons is by joining an adverb; as, *tsor*, more, very; *siṭha*, much, very, etc., to the adjective: or by using the preposition *khòta*, compared with, with the noun with which the comparison is made;

as, *thôd*, high, *tsor thôd*, higher (more high), *siṭha thôd*, highest (very high); *dānā*, clever, *tsor dānā*, more clever, *siṭha dānā*, most clever; *bôḍ*, great, *yats bôḍ*, greater (more great), *siṭha bôḍ*, greatest (most or very great): *Āftāba chhu zuni khôta bôḍ*, The sun is greater than the moon (the sun is, compared with the moon, great); *Yih gur chhu lokuṭ*, This horse is small; *Yih gur chhu tsor lokuṭ*, This horse is smaller; *Yih gur chhu siṭha lokuṭ*, This horse is very small; *Yih gur sāravai khôta chhu lokuṭ*, This horse is the smallest of all (this horse, compared with all, is small). The adverb *nihāyat* is also used with the adjective, especially by Muhammadāns; as, *Yih kul chhu hami kuli khôtạ nihāyat thôd*, This tree is very much higher than that tree; *Pira khôta chhu be-pīroi jān* (proverb), To be without a pīr is better than to have a pīr; *Yus akā kheyi tạ cheyi tạ kônsi diyi, suh chhu jān tasandi khôtạ yus ani tạ jama' kari* (proverb), Any one who eats and drinks and gives to another is better than he who brings (gathers) and collects (hoards).

CHAPTER IV.

PRONOUNS.

45. THE *first* and *second persons* of the personal pronoun have but one form for the two genders; they may be masculine or feminine, therefore, according to the gender of the nouns they represent. The genitive is inflected according to the gender and case of the noun possessed. The *third person* has a separate form for each gender in the singular, and for masculine and feminine in the plural nominative and accusative.

I. Personal Pronouns.

46. *First Person.*

Case.	Singular.	Plural.
Nom.	bȯ, bȯh, *I*	ạs, *we* and *us*
Acc.	mė, mėh, *me*	
Gen.	mion, etc., *my*	son, etc., *our*
Dat.	mė, mėh, *to me*	asi, asih, *to us*
Ag.	mė, mėh, *by me*	asi, asih, *by us*
Loc.	mė manz, *or* mėh manz, *in me*	asi manz, *or* asih manz, *in us*
Ab.	mė, mėh andarạ, *from me*	asi, asih andarạ, *from us*

47. *Second Person.*

Case.	Singular.	Plural.
Nom. *Acc.**	tsạ, *thou* and *thee*	tȯhⁱ, *you*
Gen.	chon, etc., *thy*	tuhund, etc., *your*
Dat.	tsė, tsėh, *to thee*	tȯhi, tȯhih, *to you*
Ag.	tsė, tsėh, *by thee*	tȯhi, tȯhih, *by you*
Loc.	tsė manz, *or* tsėh manz, *in thee*	tȯhi manz, *or* tȯhih manz, *in you*
Ab.	tsė, tsėh andarạ, *from thee*	tȯhi, tȯhih andarạ, *from you*

* Accusative sometimes *tsėh*, *tsė*.

48. *Third Person.*

Case	Singular.			Plural.	
	Masc.	Fem.	Neut.	Masc.	Fem.
Nom. / *Acc.*	suh, su, *he*	sȯh, sȯ, *she*	tih, ti, *it*	tim, *they*	timạ, *they*
Gen.	tạm^{i}sund, etc., tahund, etc., tasund, etc., *his, her*		tamịuk, etc., *its*	timan hund, etc., ti hund, etc., *their*	
Dat.	tamis, tas, *to him* or *her*		tath, *to it*	timan, *to them*	
Ag.	tạm^{i}, *by him*	tami, tamih, *by her*		timau, *by them*	
Loc.	tamis manz, tas manz, *in him, in her*		tath manz, *in it*	timan manz, *in them*	
Ab.	tami, tas andarạ, *from him* or *her*		tath andarạ, *from it*	timau andarạ, *from them*	

49. The third personal pronoun has often the force of a demonstrative; as, He is poor, *Suh chhu gharīb;* but, That young man is very drunk, *Suh jawān chhu sakht nashas manz.*

II. Possessive Pronouns.

50. *Mion, son, chon, tuhund, tasund,* and *timan hund,* or *ti hund*—the genitives of the personal pronouns *boh, ạs, tsạ, tȯh^{i}, suh,* and *tim*—are thus inflected—

Mion, *my*.

Case.	Masculine.		Feminine.	
	Singular noun possessed.	Plural noun possessed.	Singular noun possessed.	Plural noun possessed.
Nom. } *Acc.* }	mion	miön^{i}	miön^{i}	{ miāni, miānih
Gen.	miönis	miān^{i}ėn	miāni, miānih	miān^{i}ėn
Dat.	miönis	miān^{i}ėn	miāni, miānih	miān^{i}ėn
Ag.	miön^{i}	miān^{i}au	miāni, miānih	miān^{i}au
Loc.	miönis	miān^{i}ėn	miāni, miānih	miān^{i}ėn
Voc.	miāni, miānih	miān^{i}au	miān^{i}	miān^{i}au

51. Son, *our*.

Nom. } *Acc.* }	son	sön^{i}	sön^{i}	sāni, sānih
Gen.	sönis	sön^{i}ėn	sāni, sānih	sān^{i}ėn
Dat.	sönis	sön^{i}ėn	sāni, sānih	sān^{i}ėn
Ag.	sön^{i}	sön^{i}au	sāni, sānih	sān^{i}au
Loc.	sönis	sön^{i}ėn	sāni, sānih	sān^{i}ėn
Voc.	sāni, sānih	sān^{i}au	sān^{i}	sān^{i}au

52. Chon, *thy*.

Case.	Masculine.		Feminine.	
	Singular noun possessed.	Plural noun possessed.	Singular noun possessed.	Plural noun possessed.
Nom. *Acc.*	chon	chön^{i}	chön^{i}	chāni, chānih
Gen.	chānis	chān^{i}ēn	chāni, chānih	chān^{i}ēn
Dat.	chānis	chān^{i}ēn	chāni, chānih	chān^{i}ēn
Ag.	chön^{i}	chān^{i}au	chāni, chānih	chān^{i}au
Loc.	chānis	chān^{i}ēn	chāni, chānih	chān^{i}ēn
Voc.	chāni	chān^{i}au	chön^{i}	chān^{i}au

53. Tuhund, *your*.

Case.	Masculine Singular noun possessed.	Masculine Plural noun possessed.	Feminine Singular noun possessed.	Feminine Plural noun possessed.
Nom. *Acc.*	tuhund	tuhạnd^{i}	tuhạnz	tuhạnzạ
Gen.	tuhạndis	tuhạnd^{i}en	tuhạnzi, tuhạnzih	tuhạnzan
Dat.	tuhạndis	tuhạnd^{i}en	tuhạnzi, tuhạnzih	tuhạnzan
Ag.	tuhạnd^{i}	tuhạnd^{i}au	tuhạnzi, tuhạnzih	tuhạnz^{i}au
Loc.	tuhạndis	tuhạnd^{i}en	tuhạnzi, tuhạnzih	tuhạnzan
Voc.	tuhạndi, tuhạndih	tuhạnd^{i}au	tuhạnz^{i}	tuhạnz^{i}au

54. Tasund, *his*, *her*, *its*.

Case.	Masculine.		Feminine.	
	Singular noun possessed.	Plural noun possessed.	Singular noun possessed.	Plural noun possessed.
Nom. *Acc.*	tasund	tasạnd^{i}	tasạnz	tasạnzạ
Gen.	tasạndis	tasạnd^{i}en	tasạnzi, tasạnzih	tasạnzan
Dat.	tasạndis	tasạnd^{i}ēn	tasạnzi, tasạnzih	tasạnz^{i}an
Ag.	tasạnd^{i}	tasạnd^{i}au	tasạnzi, tasạnzih	tasạnz^{i}au
Loc.	tasạndis	tasạnd^{i}ēn	tasạnzi, tasạnzih	tasạnz^{i}an
Voc.	tasạndi, tasạndih	tasạnd^{i}au	tasạnz	tasạnz^{i}au

55. Timan hund, *or* ti hund, *their*.

Nom. *Acc.*	timan hund, *or* ti hund	timan hạnd^{i}, *or* ti hand^{i}, *or* ti hind^{i}	timan hạnz, *or* ti hanz, *or* ti hinz	timan hạnzạ, *or* ti hạnzạ, *or* ti hinzạ
Gen.	timan hạndis, *or* ti hạndis	timan hand^{i}en, *or* ti hand^{i}en, *or* ti hind^{i}en	timan hạnzī, *or* ti hanzī, *or* ti hinz^{i}	timan hạnzan, *or* ti hanzan, *or* ti hinzan

CASE.	MASCULINE.		FEMININE.	
	Singular noun possessed.	Plural noun possessed.	Singular noun possessed.	Plural noun possessed.
Dat.	timan hạndis, *or* ti hạndis	timan han-d^{i}en, *or* ti hand^{i}-en, *or* ti hind^{i}en	timan hạnzī, *or* ti hanzī, *or* ti hinz^{i}	timan hạn-zan, *or* ti hanzan, *or* ti hin-zan
Ag.	timan hạnd^{i}, *or* ti hạnd^{i}	timan hạn-d^{i}au, *or* ti hạnd^{i}-au, *or* ti hind^{i}au	timan hạnz^{i}, *or* ti hanz^{i}, *or* ti hinzi	timan hạn-z^{i}au, *or* ti hanz^{i}-au, *or* ti hinz^{i}au
Loc.	timan hạndis, *or* ti hạndis	timan hạn-d^{i}èn, *or* ti handi-èn, *or* ti hindièn	timan hạnz^{i}, *or* ti hanz^{i}, *or* ti hinzi	timan hạn-zan, *or* ti hanzan, *or* ti hin-zan
Voc.	timan hạndi, timan hạn-dih, *or* ti hạndi, ti hạndih	timan han-d^{i}au, *or* ti hand^{i}-au, *or* ti hind^{i}au	timan hạnz, *or* ti hanz, *or* ti hinz	timan hạn-z^{i}au, *or* ti hanz^{i}-au, *or* ti hinz^{i}au

56. When the possessive pronoun accompanies a noun in the genitive case with *-uk*, the final *s* of the possessive pronoun is omitted, and in the first and second persons the vowel is slightly modified; as, *sāni kalamuk, chāni kalamuk, tasandi kalamuk.* For further particulars, *vide* Syntax: Genitive case.

57. PRONOMINAL AFFIXES AS USED WITH VERBS.

PERSON.	SINGULAR.			PLURAL.
	Acc. for pres. and fut., and Ag. for past tenses.	Acc. for past tense.	Dat. for all tenses.	Ag. Acc. Dat.
1st	-m	-s	-m	—
2nd	-t (i)	-k	-i	-va
3rd	-n (s)	-n	-s	-k

For more details concerning pronominal affixes, see Verb.

III. DEMONSTRATIVE PRONOUNS.

58. The third personal pronoun is often used as a demonstrative in Kashmīrī, as well as *yih* and *huh*. Of the latter two pronouns, *yih* refers to an object that is near, or to the last of two objects mentioned in conversation, whilst *huh* is used of an object more remote.

59. Yih, *this*.

CASE.	SINGULAR.	PLURAL.
Nom. } *Acc.* }	yih, *this*	yim, fem. yima̤, *these*
Gen.	yėmⁱ sund, etc., neut. yetⁱuk, etc., *of this*	yiman hund, etc., *or* yihund, etc., *of these*
Dat.	yėmis, neut. yath, yėth, *to this*	yiman, *to these*
Ag.	yėmⁱ, fem. yemi, yemih, *this*	yiman, *these*
Loc.	yėmis nish, fem. yemi *or* yemih nish, *near this*	yiman andar, *in these*
Voc.	hā yėmis, *O this*	hā yimau, *O these*

60. Instead of the above declension, the following is often used, especially by villagers :—

CASE.	SINGULAR.	PLURAL.
Nom. } *Acc.* }	yih, fem. nòh, *this*	nòm^{i}, fem. nòmạ, *these*
Gen.	nòm^{i} sund, etc., *or* nạm-sund, etc., *of this*	nòman hund, *or* nuhund, *of these*
Dat.	nòmis, neut. yath, yòth, *to this*	nòman, *to these*
Ag.	nòm^{i}, fem. nòmi, nòmih, *this*	nòmau, *these*
Loc.	nòmis nish, fem. nòmi *or* nòmih nish, *near this*	nòman nish, *near these*
Voc.	ha nòmis, hā nòmih, *O this*	hā nòmau, *O these*

61. Huh, *that*.

Nom. } *Acc.* }	hu, huh, fem. hò, hòh, *that*	ạm^{i}, *those*
Gen.	ạm sund, etc., *of that*	aman hund, etc., *of those*
Dat.	ạmis, neut. ath, *to that*	aman, *to those*
Ag.	ạmi, fem. ami, amih, *that*	amau, *those*
Loc.	ạmis nish, fem. ami *or* amih nish, *near that*	aman nish, *near those*
Voc.	hā ạmis, fem. hā ami *or* amih, *O that*	hā amau, *O those*

62. The pronoun *huh* is very frequently used by women in speaking of any one (particularly men) whose name they do not wish to mention.

IV. Reflexive Pronouns.

63. The word *pānạ* in Kashmīrī means "self," and is in declinable; it is used with all persons, numbers, and genders; as, *bo pānạ*, I myself; *ạs panạ*, we ourselves; *tsạ pānạ*, thou thyself; *tŏh^{i} pānạ*, you yourselves; *tim pānạ*, they themselves, etc. The intensive form of *pānạ* is *pānai*.

64. *Pān* means "the human body," and hence "self." We can say, for instance, *Mion pān chhu bimār*, My body is ill. *Pānawön^{i}* means "amongst ourselves, yourselves, themselves," etc., like *āpas meṇ* in Urdu. *Pānạ* is not used in an honorific sense, as *āp* is in Urdu.

65. Panun, *oẉn*, is thus declined—

Case.	Singular.		Plural.	
	Masc.	Fem.	Masc.	Fem.
Nom. *Acc.*	panun	panaṇ^{i}	panaṇ^{i}	panaṇi
Gen.	panaṇ^{i} sund, etc., *or* pananisạk sund, etc.	panaṇi sanz, etc.	panaṇ^{i} sund, etc.	panaṇi sanzạ, etc.
Dat.	panaṇis	panaṇi	panaṇ^{i}ēn	panaṇ^{i}ēn
Ag.	panaṇ^{i}	panaṇi	panaṇ^{i}au	panaṇ^{i}au
Loc.	panaṇis	panaṇi	panaṇ^{i}ēn	panaṇ^{i}ēn
Voc.	hā panaṇis	hā panaṇi	hā panaṇ^{i}au	hā panaṇ^{i}au

66. *Panun* is used in Kashmīrī like *apnā* in Urdu. It constantly supplies the place of "my," "thy," "his," "her," "our," "your," "their," when they represent the same person as the nominative of the sentence.

67. *Panun pān* and *panani pānạ*, my own self, myself, himself, etc., are regularly inflected; thus, *Suh chhu panun pān mārān*, He is killing himself; *Tsạ chhuk pananis pānas taklif diwān*, Thou art giving thyself trouble; *Panani pānuk gam*, My own sorrow.

68. When the pronouns "my," "thy," etc., do not represent the same person as the nominative of the sentence in which they stand, they cannot be expressed by *panun;* the genitive of the personal pronoun must then be used; thus, *Suh chhu panani kitāb parān*, He is reading his (own) book; *Suh chhu tasạnz kitāb parān*, He is reading his (another person's) book.

V. The Relative Pronoun.

69. Yus, *who.*

Case.	Singular.	Plural.
Nom. *Acc.*	yus, fem. yòsa, *who;* neut. yih, *or* yi, *which*	yim, *who, which, that*
Gen.	yèmⁱsund, etc., *or* yasund, etc., *whose*	yiman hund, etc., *or* yi-hund, etc., *of whom, which*
Dat.	yas, *or* yèmis, *to whom;* neut. yath, *or* yèth, *to what*	yiman, *to whom, which*
Ag.	yèmⁱ, fem. yèmi, *or* yèmih, *who, which*	yiman, *who*
Loc.	yèmis nish, fem. yèmi *or* yèmih nish, *near whom, which*	yiman nish, *near whom, which*

70. The relative pronoun *yus* is generally followed by the personal pronoun *suh*, and agrees with its substantive

(expressed or understood) in number, gender, and case; thus, *Yiman nechiv'en chhė himmat tim hechan*, Those boys who have ambition, they will learn; *Yôsą kur māji chhė mānān so sapani māji hish*, The daughter who obeys (her) mother, she will become like (her) mother; *Yih chhu wanān tih chhu karān*, What he says, that he does.

71. The pronoun *suh* may be also used with the antecedent, and the relative will then follow; as, *Mė nish chhė sò mīlidavāt yòsa tòhi nish ös*, I have the inkstand which you had.

VI. The Interrogative Pronoun.

72. Kus? *who?*

Case.	Singular.	Plural.
Nom. / *Acc.*	kus? fem. kòsa? *who?* neut. kya? *what?*	kam? fem. kamą? *who? which? what?*
Gen.	kąm'sund, etc.? *or* kasund, etc.? *or* kòhund, etc.? *whose?* neut. kam'uk, etc.? *of what?*	kaman hund, etc.? *whose?*
Dat.	kamis *or* kas? *to whom?* neut. kath? *to what?*	kaman? *to whom, which, what?*
Ag.	kam'? *who?* fem. kami? *what?*	kamau? *who? which? what?*
Loc.	kamis nish? *near whom?* neut. kath nish? *near what?*	kaman nish? *near whom, which, what?*

VII. Indefinite Pronouns.

73. Kaṇh, *any*; kėṇh, *some*.

Case.	Singular.	Plural.
Nom. *Acc.*	kaṇh, neut. kėṇh, *any*	kėṇh, *some*
Gen.	könsi hund, etc., kunʼuk, *of any*	kėṇtsan hund, etc., *of some*
Dat.	köṇsi, *to any*	kėṇtsan, *to some*
Ag.	köṇsi, *any*	kėṇtsau, *some*

74. It will be observed that *kėṇh* is both the sing. neut. of *kaṇh*, meaning "something;" and also the plu. masc., fem., and neut., meaning "some persons or things."

75. To the above may be added *akā*, one; *bėyāk*, another; *kaṇsa* or *kāṇtsa*, *kustām*, some one; *kėṇsa*, or *kėṇtsa*, something.

76. *Akā* and *bėyāk* are declined like nouns of the first declension; and *kustām* is declined regularly like *kus*, with *tām* added.

VIII. Distributive Pronouns.

77. These are *har*, each; *prat*, each, every; *soroi*, *sorai*, or *sorsai*, all.

78. IX. Adjective Pronouns.

Singular.		Plural.	
Masc.	Fem.	Masc.	Fem.
yuth, *like this*	yits	yith^{i}	yitsạ
tiuth, *like that*	tits	tith^{i}	titsạ
kiuth? *like what?*	kits?	kith^{i}?	kitsạ?
yut, *this much* or *many*	yīts	yīt^{i}	yītsạ
tut, *that much* or *many*	tīts	tīt^{i}	tītsạ
kut (kot, kats)? *how much* or *many?*	kạts (kits)?	kạt^{i} (kīt^{i})?	katsạ (kītsa)?

For other forms, as, *yȯt*, here; *katitām*, somewhere; *yiti*, just here; *yati*, just where; see Adverb.

X. Compound Pronouns.

79. There are a large number of compound pronouns in Kashmīrī, formed by combining together in various ways the simple pronouns already mentioned. They are for the most part of the indefinite kind, and follow the inflections of the simple forms of which they are composed; as, *yus kāṇh*, whoever; gen. *yas kȫṇsi hund*; dat. *yas kȫṇsi*, etc.

The most common and useful are: *Yikẹṇh*, or *yih kẹṇh*, whatever; *yus akā*, whoever; *bėyih kaṇh*, some one else; *bėyih kẹṇh*, something else; *kāṇh nạ*, no one; *kẹṇh nạ*, nothing; *kaṇh nata kaṇh*, some one or other; *kyatām*, something; *kẹṇh nata kẹṇh*, something or other; *prat kaṇh, har kaṇh*, every one; *har akā*, every one; *prat kẹṇh, har kẹṇh*, everything; *bėyih na*, no more; *bėyih sorȯi*, all the rest; *bėyih sitha*, much more; *vāraya*, several; *ada kya*, what else (of course).

80. INTENSIVE FORMS. Almost all the pronouns can be made intensive by adding to them ī, *ai*, *oi*, or *öi*; as, *boi*, *boī*; *ạs*, *ạsī*; *su*, *suī*; *toh*[i], *tohī*; *chon*, *chonoi*; *hu*, *huī*; *yih*, *yihoi*, fem. *yihai*; *yus*, *yusoi*; *yuth*, *yuthoi*; *yem*[i]*sund*, *yem*[i]*sundoi*.

CHAPTER V.

VERBS.

81. THE verbs in Kashmīrī are generally very regular. All infinitives invariably end in *-un*, and, by rejecting the final *-un*, we have the root; as, *āsun*, to be, root *ās*; *pakun*, to go, walk, root *pak*; *mārun*, to beat, kill, root *mār*. The root is always the second person imperative, to which the regular affixes are added for the other persons of the imperative mood. By adding *-ān* to the root, we obtain the indefinite active participle, as *āsān*, *pakān*, *mārān*, being, going, killing; by adding *-it* to the root, the conjunctive participle, as *āsit*, *pakit*, *mārit*, having been, gone, killed; and by adding *-öni*, the adverbial participle, as *āsöni*, *paköni*, *māröni*, on being, on going, on killing. The future is formed by adding the regular affixes *-ạ*, *-ak*, *-i*, etc., to the root, as *āsạ*, *āsak*, *āsi*, I shall be, thou wilt be, he will be; so *pakạ*, *pakak*, *paki*; *mārạ*, *mārak*, *māri*. The past subjunctive is formed by adding the regular affixes *-ahạ*, *-ahak*, *-ihe*, etc., to the root; as, *āsahạ*, *āsahak*, *āsihe*, I might have been *or* had I been, thou mightest have been, he might have been; so *pakahạ*, *pakahak*, *pakihe*; *mārahạ*, *mārahak*, *mārihe*. The noun of agency is formed from the root by adding *-anwol* or *-awun*; as, *āsanwol*, *āsawun*, one who is, *or* is about to be; so *pakanwol*, *pakawun*, a goer, *or* one about to go; *māranwol*, *mārawun*, a killer. A pluperfect, sometimes

used, is also formed from the root, but often with a change of the last consonant; as, *āsos*, *āsok*, *āsov*, etc., I had been, thou hadst been, he had been; *pachos*, *pachok*, *pachịov*, etc., I had gone, thou hadst gone, he had gone. The transitive verb *mārun* makes the pluperf. masc. sing. *māriov*, fem. *māreyi*, etc.

82. To form the third person masculine singular of the past indefinite, the vowel of the root generally undergoes a slight change. Of these changes the most simple are—long *a* is changed into long *o*, and short *a* into short *o*; thus, *āsun*, to be, root *ās*, 3rd pers. sing. masc. past indef. *os*, he was; so *mārun*, *mār*, 3rd pers. sing. masc. past indef. *mor*, he killed; *pakun*, *pak*, *pȯk*, he went. From the third person singular masculine past indefinite the perfect participle is formed by adding *-mut*; as, *osmut*, been; *pȯkmut*, gone; *mormut*, killed.

All the other tenses in the conjugation of transitive and intransitive verbs are formed by the help of the auxiliary verb *āsun*.

83. The following example will show how the principal parts of the verb are formed from the root:—

Infinitive: Pakun, *to go.*

Root: pak	pak,	2nd pers. sing. imp.
	pakān,	act. part.
	pakit,	conjunc. part.
	pakȯni,	adverb. part.
	pakạ,	1st pers. sing. fut.
	pakahạ,	1st pers. sing. past subjunc.
	pakanwol,	nouns of agency
	pakawun,	nouns of agency
	pachiov,	3rd pers. masc. sing. pluperf.
(pak) pȯk	pȯk,	3rd pers. masc. sing. past indef.
	pȯkmut,	perf. part.

CONJUGATION OF VERBS.

84. Āsun, *to be.*

Root: ās (chh).

Infinitive: āsun, *to be.*
āsaṇa, *on account of being.*
āsani, *in order to be.*
āsanuk, etc., *of being* (declined).

Present participle: āsān, *being.*
Conjunctive participle: āsit, *having been* (not declined).
Adverbial participle: āsöni, *on being* (not declined).
Past participle: osmut, *been* (declined).

	SINGULAR.		PLURAL.	
	Masc.	Fem.	Masc.	Fem.
Nouns of agency	āsanwol, *he who is* or *is about to be*	āsanwöj	āsanwölⁱ	āsanwājeni
	āsawun, *he who is* or *is about to be*	āsawaṇⁱ	āsawaṇⁱ	āsawani
Past participle	osmut, *been*	ösmats	ösmatⁱ	āsamatsa

INDICATIVE MOOD.

Present (indefinite): *I am*, etc.

SINGULAR.		PLURAL.	
Masc.	Fem.	Masc.	Fem.
Bȯ, Bȯh } chhus	bȯ, bȯh } chhas	ạs {chhi, chhih	ạs {chhė, chhėh
Tsạ chhuk	tsạ chhak	tȯhi chhivạ	tȯhi chhėvạ
Su, Suh } chhu, chhuh	sȯ, sȯh } chhė, chheh	tim {chhi, chhih	timạ {chhė, chhėh

Past (indefinite): *I was*, etc.

Bȯ osus	bȯ ösạs	ạs ösi	ạs āsạ
Tsạ osuk	tsạ ösạk	tȯhi ösivạ	tȯhi āsavạ
Su os	sȯ ös	tim ösi	timạ āsạ

Pluperfect: *I had been*, etc. (not often used).

Bȯ āsos, *or* āsyos	bȯ āseyas, *or* āseyes	ạs āsey	ạs āseyi
Tsạ āsok, *or* āsyok	tsạ aseyak, *or* āseyek	tȯhi āsėvạ	tȯhi āseyivạ
Su āsov, *or* āsyov	sȯ āseyi, *or* aseyih	tim āsey	timạ āseyi, *or* aseyih

Future: *I shall be, thou wilt be*, etc.

SINGULAR.		PLURAL.	
Bȯ	āsạ	ạs	āsau
Tsạ	āsak	tȯh^{i}	āsiv
Su, Sȯ	āsi, āsih	tim, timạ	āsan

IMPERATIVE MOOD.

Be thou, etc.

Tsạ	ās, āstạ	tȯh^{i}	ösiu, östau
Su, Sȯ	ösin, östan	tim, timạ	ösin, östan

SUBJUNCTIVE MOOD.

Present: *I may*, etc.

Bȯ āsạ, etc., *or* Bȯ ai āsạ *or* āsạhai, *if I may*, etc., the same as the Indicative Future.

Past (indefinite): *were I*, or *had I been*, etc.

Bȯ	āsahạ	ạs	āsahau
Tsạ	āsahak	tȯh^{i}	āsihiu
Su	āsihe	tim	āsahan

Interrogative Forms.

Present: *am I?* etc.

Singular.		Plural.	
Masc.	Fem.	Masc.	Fem.
Bȯ chhusạ?	bȯ chhasa?	ạs chhiā?	ạs chhēā?
Tsạ chhukạ?	tsạ chhaka?	tȯhⁱ chhivā?	tȯhⁱ chhēvạ?
Su {chhuā? chhwā? chhā?}	sȯ chheā?	tim chhiā?	timạ chhēā?

Future: *shall I be?* etc.

Singular.		Plural.	
Bȯ	āsā?	ạs	āsạvā?
Tsạ	āsakā?	tȯhⁱ	āsivā?
Su	āsiā?	tim	āsanā?

85. The interrogative forms are the present, future, etc., with *ạ*, *a*, *ā*, added to the various persons of the indicative mood.

Other tenses are formed from the above, as—

Present imperfect: Bȯ chhus āsān, etc., *I am being;* the participle remaining uninflected.

Past imperfect: Bȯ osus āsān, etc., *I was being.*

Future imperfect: Bȯ āsạ āsān, etc., *I shall be being.*

Present perfect: Bȯ chhus osmut, etc., *I have been.*

Past perfect (pluperfect): Bȯ osus osmut, etc., *I had been.*

Future perfect: Bȯ āsạ osmut, etc., *I shall have been.*

86. The perf. part. *osmut* is declined to agree with its nominative in number and gender, as follows:—

SINGULAR.		PLURAL.	
Masc.	Fem.	Masc.	Fem.
Bó chhus osmut	bó chhas ösmạts	ạs chhi ösmạt^{i}	ạs chhė āsamatsa
Tsạ chhuk osmut	tsạ chhak ösmạts	tóh^{i} chhivạ ösmat^{i}	tóh^{i} chhėvạ āsạmatsạ
Su chhu osmut	só chhė ösmạts	tim chhi ösmat^{i}	timạ chhė āsạmatsạ

Osmut is declined in the same way, with the various persons of *osus* for the pluperfect, and of *āsạ* for the future perfect; also with *āsahạ* of the subjunctive mood.

87. *Conditional mood.* This is generally formed by the help of *ai*, if, which is sometimes added to the verb as an affix; as, *Su ai mari* (or *marihai*) *tạ bo kya karạ?* If he should die then, what shall I do? *Tam^{i} ai tas zahr diutmut āsihė tạ su marihė zarur*, If he had given him poison he would certainly have died.

88. The verb *āsun* is the only one in the language that has a present indefinite tense; the others have only a present imperfect, or continuous.

89. *Imperative mood.* The second forms given above are more respectful than the first; *āstạ* is more respectful than *ās*. Besides these, others are also used, obtained by adding *zi*, *sa* (from *sāhib*), *shā* (from *bādshāh*), *haz* (from *hazrat*), to the simple imperative; as, *kar*, do thou; *karsa*, be pleased to do, *or* do, sir; *karshā* (very respectful), do, O king.

90. **INTRANSITIVE VERBS.**

(1) Pakun, *to go, to walk.*
Root: pak.

Infinitive: pakun, *to go.*
pakanạ, *on account of going, for going.*
pakani, *in order to go.*
pakanuk, *of going.*

Active participle: pakān, *going.*
Conjunctive participle: pakit, *having gone.*
Adverbial participle: pakönị, *on going, at the time of going.*
Perfect participle: pòkmut, *gone.*
Nouns of agency: {pakanwol, pakawun,} *a goer, one who goes* or *is about to go.*

INDICATIVE MOOD.

Present (imperfect, or continuous): *I am going*, etc.

SINGULAR.				PLURAL.			
Masc.		Fem.		Masc.		Fem.	
Bò chhus		bò chhas		ạs chhi		ạs chhė	
Tsạ chhuk	pakān	tsạ chhak	pakān	tòh^{i} chhi-vạ	pakān	tòh^{i} chhė-vạ	pakān
Su chhu		sò chhė		tim chhi		timạ chhė	

Imperfect: *I was going*, etc.

Masc.		Fem.		Masc.		Fem.	
Bò osus		bò ösạs		ạs ös^{i}		ạs āsạ	
Tsạ osuk	pakān	tsạ ösạk	pakān	tòh^{i} ös^{i}vạ	pakān	tòh^{i} āsavạ	pakān
Su os		sò ös		tim ös^{i}		timạ āsạ	

Perfect: *I have gone*, etc.

Singular.		Plural.	
Masc.	Fem.	Masc.	Fem.
Bò chhus	bò chhas	ạs chhi	ạs chhė
Tsạ chhuk	tsạ chhak	tòh^i chhi-vạ	tòh^i chhė-vạ
Su chhu	sò chhė	tim chhi	timạ chhė
} pòkmut	} pachmats	} pakmạt^i	} pachmạtsa

Past (indefinite): *I went*, etc.

Bò pòkus	bò { pachis, pachės	ạs pak^i	ạs pachi
Tsạ pòkuk	tsạ { pachik, pachėk	tòh^i { pakiva, pakėva	tòh^i pachiva
Su pòk	sò pạch	tim pak^i	timạ pachi

Pluperfect—1st form: *I had gone*, etc. (used also as Subjunctive).

Bò pachos, *or* pachyos	bò pacheyas, *or* pacheyės	ạs pachey	ạs pacheyi
Tsạ pachok, *or* pachyok	tsạ pacheyėk	tòh^i pacheva	tòh^i pacheyi-va
Su pachiov, *or* pachyov	sò pacheyi	tim pachey	timạ pacheyi

Pluperfect—2nd form: *I had gone*, etc. (more often used).

Singular						Plural					
Masc.			Fem.			Masc.			Fem.		
Bò	osus	pòkmut	bò	ösạs	pachnats	ạs	ös'	pakmatị	ạs	āsạ	pachmatsạ
Tsạ	osuk		tsạ	ösạk		tòh'	ös'va		tòh'	āsavạ	
Su	os		sò	ös		tim	ös'		timạ	āsạ	

Future: *I shall go*, etc.

Singular		Plural	
Bò	pakạ	ạs	pakau
Tsạ	pakak	tòh'	pakiu
Su, Sò	paki	tim, timạ	pakan

Future Imperfect (or continuous): *I shall be going*, etc.

Singular			Plural		
Bò	āsạ	pakān	ạs	āsau	pakān
Tsạ	āsak		tòh'	āsiu	
Su, Sò	āsi		tim, timạ	āsan	

Future Perfect: *I shall have gone*, etc.

Singular.				Plural.			
Masc.		Fem.		Masc.		Fem	
Bô āsạ	pôkmut	bô āsạ	pachmats	ạs āsau	pakmatʲ	ạs āsau	pachmatsa
Tsạ āsak		tsạ āsak		tôhʲ āsiv		tôhʲ āsiv	
Su āsi		sô āsi		tim āsan		timạ āsan	

IMPERATIVE MOOD.

Go thou, etc.

	Singular.			Plural.	
	Masc. and Fem.	Respectful. Masc. and Fem.		Masc. and Fem.	Respectful. Masc. and Fem.
Tsạ	pak	pakta̩, pak-sa; pakzi, pak-shā	tôhʲ	pakiu, paki-heu	pakiusa, paktau, pachtau (fem.)
Su, Sô	pakin	pakitan	tim, timạ	pakin	pạkitan

"Let me, him, them, etc., go" ("give me, him, them, to ... may be thus expressed (*di* is the 2nd pers. sing. imp. ... give)—

Singular.		Plural.	
Mė Tsė Tas	di, diu, etc., pakanạ	asi tȯhi timan	di, diu, etc., pakanạ

Subjunctive Mood.

Present: *if I go*, etc.

Bȯ	pakahai, *or* ai pakạ	ạs	pakavai, *or* ai pakau
Tsạ	pakakai, *or* ai pakak	tȯhi	pakivai, *or* ai pakiu
Su Sȯ	pakei, *or* ai paki	tim timạ	pakanai, *or* ai pakan

Past (indefinite): *had I gone*, etc., *if I went*, etc.

Bȯ	pakahạ, *or* ai pakahạ	ạs	pakahau, *or* ai paka-hau
Tsạ	pakahak, *or* ai pakahak	tȯhi	pakihiu, *or* ai paki-hiu
Su Sȯ	pakihe, *or* ai pakihe	tim timạ	pakahan, *or* ai paka-han

Perfect: *I may have gone*, etc.

Bȯ āsạ pȯkmut, fem. bȯ āsạ pȯkmats, etc., the same as the future perfect. By adding *ai* or *harga*, Bȯ ai āsạ pȯkmut, *or* Bȯ āsahai pȯkmut, *If I may have gone.*

Pluperfect: *I might have gone*, etc.

Singular.		Plural.	
Masc.	**Fem.**	**Masc.**	**Fem.**
Bȯ āsahạ	bȯ āsahạ	ạs āsahau	ạs āsahau
Tsạ āsahak	tsạ āsahak	tȯh^{i} āsihiu	tọh^{i} āsihiu
Su āsihe	sȯ āsihe	tim asahan	timạ asahan
} pōkmut	} pachmats	} pakmat^{i}	} pachmatsa

Interrogative Forms.

Present: *am I going?* etc.

Bȯ chhusạ	bȯ chhasa	ạs chhiā	ạs chhėā
Tsạ chhuka	tsạ chhaka	tȯh^{i} chhi-vā	tȯh^{i} chhė-vā
Su {chhuā, chhwā, chhā	sȯ chhėā	tim chhiā	timạ chhėā
} pakān?	} pakān?	} pakān?	} pakān?

Future: *shall I go?* etc.

Singular.		Plural.	
Bȯ	pakā?	ạs	pakavā?
Tsạ	pakakā?	tȯh^{i}	pakivā?
Su } Sȯ }	pakiā?	tim } timạ }	pakanā?

So of the other tenses—

Bȯ chhusạ pȯkmut? *have I gone?*
Bȯ osusa pȯkmut? *had I gone?*
Bȯ āsā pakān? *shall I be going?*
Bȯ āsā pȯkmut? *shall I have gone?*

91. (2) Dorun, *to run.*

Root: dor.

Infinitive: dorun, *to run.*
dorana, *for running.*
dorani, *in order to run.*
doranuk, etc., *of running.*

Active participle: dorān, *or* dawān, *running.*

Conjunctive participle: dorit, *having run.*

Adverbial participle: dorön^i, *on running.*

Perfect participle: doryomut, *or* durmut, *run.*

Nouns of agency: { doranwol, *a runner.* / dorawun, *one about to run.* }

INDICATIVE MOOD.

Present (regular): *I am running*, etc.

Bȯ chhus, bȯ chhas dorān *or* dawān, etc.

Imperfect (regular): *I was running*, etc.

Bȯ osus, bȯ osạs dorān *or* dawān, etc.

Past (indefinite): *I ran*, etc.

SINGULAR.		PLURAL.	
Masc.	Fem.	Masc.	Fem.
Bȯ doryos	bȯ doreyas, *or* doreyes	ạs dorei, *or* dorey	ạs doreyi
T̲sạ doryok	t̲sạ doreyek	tȯh^i doreva	tȯh^i doreyiva
Su doryov	sȯ doreyi	tim dorei, *or* dorey	timạ doreyi

Perfect (regular): *I have run*, etc.

Bò chhus, bò chhas doryomut *or* durmut, etc.

Pluperfect—1st form: *I had run*, etc.

Singular.		Plural.	
Masc.	Fem.	Masc.	Fem.
Bò doreyos	bò {doreyeyas, doreyeyes}	ạs doreyey	ạs doreyeyi
Tsạ doreyok	tsạ doreyeyek	tòh^{i} doreyeva	tòh^{i} doreyiva
Su doreyov	sò doreyeyi	tim doreyey	timạ doreyeyi

Pluperfect—2nd form (regular): *I, we, had run*, etc.
Bò osus doryomut *or* durmut, bò öṣas doremats *or* durmats.
Ạs ös^{i} doremạt^{i} *or* durimat^{i}, ạs äsạ dorematsa *or* dorimatsa, etc.

Future (regular): *I, thou, he* or *she will run*, etc.

Bò dorạ, tsạ dorak, su *or* sò dori, etc.

Imperative Mood (regular).

Run thou, etc.

Tsạ dor, dorta, etc.

Subjunctive Mood.

Present (regular): *if I run* or *may run*, etc.

Bò ai dora, etc.

Past (regular): *had I run*, etc.

Bò doraha, etc.

92. (3) Gatshun, *to go, to become.*

Root: gatsh.

Infinitive: gatshun, *to go, to become.*
gatshana, *for going.*
gatshani, *in order to go.*
gatshanuk, etc., *of going.*

Active participle: gatshān, *going.*

Conjunctive participle: gatshit, *having gone.*

Adverbial participle: gatshöni, *on going.*

Perfect participle: gomut, *gone, become.*

Nouns of agency: gatshanwol, *a goer.* gatshawun, *one about to go.*

INDICATIVE MOOD.

Present, Imperfect, and Perfect, regular.

Past (indefinite): *I went* or *became*, etc.

Singular.		Plural.	
Masc.	Fem.	Masc.	Fem.
Bò gos	bò gāyas, *or* gāyes	ạs gāi, *or* gāy	ạs gāyi
Tsạ gok	tsạ gāyek	tòhi gava	tòhi gāyiva
Su gāw	sò gāyi	tim gāi, *or* gāy	timạ gāyi

Pluperfect—1st form: *I had gone* or *become*, etc.

Bò gāyos	bò gāyeyas, *or* gāyeyes	ạs gāyey	ạs gāyeyi
Tsạ gāyok	tsạ gāyeyek	tòhi gāyèva	tòhi gāyiva
Su gāyov	sò gāyeyi	tim gāyey	timạ gāyeyi

The other parts of this verb present no difficulty. They are conjugated like *pakun.*

93. (4) Sapun, *or* sapanun, *to become.*

Root: sapan.

Infinitive: sapun (sapanun), *to become.*

sapanuk, etc., *of becoming.*

Active participle: sapanān, *becoming.*

Conjunctive participle: sapanit, *having become.*

Past participle: sapanmut, *become.*

Nouns of agency: {sapanwol, sapawun,} *one who becomes* or *is about to become.*

INDICATIVE MOOD.

Present (imperfect): *I am becoming*, etc.

Bò chhus, bò chhas sapanān, etc.

Imperfect: *I was becoming*, etc.

Bò osus, bò öṣas sapanān, etc.

Perfect: *I have become*, etc.

Bò chhus, bò chhas sapanmut, sapanmats, etc.

Past (indefinite): *I became*, etc.

Bò sapanus; tsa̱ sapanuk; ạs sapaṇi, etc.

Pluperfect—1st form: *I had become*, etc.

Bò sapan'os, *or* sapanyos; tsa̱ sapan'ok, *or* sapanyok; ạs sapaney, *or* sapanei, etc.

Pluperfect—2nd form: *I had become*, etc.

Bò osus, bò öṣas sapanmut, etc.

Future: *I shall become*, etc.

Bȯ sapaṅạ; t̲s̲ạ sapanak; ạs sapanau, etc.

Future Imperfect: *I shall be becoming*, etc.

Bȯ āsạ sapanān; t̲s̲ạ āsak sapanān, etc.

Future Perfect: *I shall have become*, etc.

Bȯ āsạ sapanmut; t̲s̲ạ āsak sapanmut, etc.

Imperative Mood:

Become thou, etc.

T̲s̲ạ sapan, sapantạ; su sapanin, etc.

Subjunctive Mood.

Present: *if I may become*, etc.

Bȯ ai sápanạ; t̲s̲ạ ai sapanak, etc.

Past: *had I become*, etc.

Bȯ sapanahạ; t̲s̲ạ sapanahak, etc.

Perfect: *I may have become*, etc.

Bȯ āsạ sapanmut; t̲s̲ạ āsak sapanmut, etc.

The verb *sapadun* also means "to become," and is often used for *sapun*.

The principal parts of *sapadun* are: *Sapadun; sapad; sapadān; sapadit; sapȯdmut; sapadus; sapanyos.*

The verb is regular.

It must be remembered that the *d* changes into *z* in the feminine; as, *bȯ sapadus* (masc.), *bȯ sapazas* (fem.); *su sapud* (masc.), *sȯ sapaz* (fem.); *sapȯdmut* (masc.), *sapazmat̲s̲* (fem.).

TRANSITIVE VERBS.

94. (1) Karun, *to do, to make.*

Root: kar.

Infinitive: karun, *to do.*
karaṇa, *for doing.*
karani, *to do, in order to do.*
karanuk, *of doing.*

Active participle: karān, *doing.*

Conjunctive participle: karit, *having done.*

Adverbial participle: karönⁱ, *on doing, at the time of doing.*

Perfect participle: kòrmut, *done.*

Nouns of agency: { karanwol, karawun, } *a doer, one who is about to do.*

INDICATIVE MOOD.

Present (imperfect, or continuous): *I am doing*, etc.

SINGULAR.				PLURAL.			
Masc.		Fem.		Masc.		Fem.	
Bò chhus Tsa̱ chhuk Su chhu	karān	bò chhas tsa̱ chhak sò chhė	karān	a̱s chhi tòhⁱ chhiva tim chhi	karān	a̱s chhė tòhⁱ chhė-va̱ tima̱ chhė	karān

Imperfect: *I was doing*, etc.

Masc.		Fem.		Masc.		Fem.	
Bò osus Tsa̱ osuk Su os	karān	bò ösa̱s tsa̱ ösa̱k sò ös	karān	a̱s ösⁱ tòhⁱ ösⁱva̱ tim ösⁱ	karān	a̱s āsa̱ tòhⁱ āsava̱ tima̱ āsa̱	karān

Past (indefinite): *I did*, etc. (properly *it*, *he*, *she*, etc., *was done by me*, etc.).

	Singular.		Plural.	
	Masc.	Fem.	Masc.	Fem.
Mė, Asi, Tạmⁱ, Tami, Timau	kȯr *	kạr *	karⁱ *	kari *
T̲sė	kȯrut	kạrat	karit	karit
Tȯhi	kȯrvạ	kạrvạ	kạrⁱva	kariva

Perfect: *I have done*, etc. (*it*, *he*, *she*, etc., *was done by me*, etc.).

Mė, Asi, Tạmⁱ, Tami, Timau	chhu kȯr-mut	chhė kar-mat̲s	chhi karⁱ-matⁱ	chhė kari-mat̲sa
T̲sė	chhut kȯr-mut	chhėt kar-mat̲s	chhit karⁱ-matⁱ	chhėt kari-mat̲sa
Tȯhi	chhuva kȯr-mut	chhėva kar-mat̲s	chhiva karⁱ-matⁱ	chhėva kari-mat̲sa

* Always agreeing in gender and number with what would be the objective in English.

Pluperfect—1st form: *I had done* or *had I done it, he, she*, etc. (used also as Past Subjunctive).

Mė, Asi, Tạm^{i}, Tami, Timau	kariov, *or* karyov, *or* kareyov	kạrey, *or* ka-reyey	karey, *or* kareyey	kareyi, *or* kareyeyi
Tsė	kariot, *or* karyot, *or* kareyot	kariet, *or* karyet, *or* kareyet	kariet, *or* karyet, *or* kareyet	kareyit, *or* kareyeyit
Tôhi	kariovạ, *or* karyova, *or* kare-yova	kareyva, *or* kareyėva	kareyva, *or* kareyeva	kareyivạ

Pluperfect—2nd form: *I had done*, etc. (*it, he, she*, etc., *was done by me*, etc.).

	Singular.		Plural.	
	Masc.	Fem.	Masc.	Fem.
Mė, Asi, Tạm^{i}, Tami, Timau	os kòrmut	ös karmats	ös^{i} kar^{i}mat^{i}	āsạ kar^{i}-matsạ
Tsė	osut kòrmut	ösạt kar-mats	ösit kar^{i}mat^{i}	āsat kar^{i}-matsạ
Tòhi	osva kòrmut	ösva kar-mats	os^{i}va kar^{i}-mat^{i}	āsava kar^{i}-matsạ

Future: *I will do*, etc.; used also as Present Subjunctive: *I may do*, etc.

Singular.		Plural.	
Bȯ	kara̤	a̤s	karau
T̲s̲a̤	karak	tȯh^{i}	kariv
Su } Sȯ }	kari	tim } tima̤ }	karan

Future Imperfect (or continuous): *I*, etc., *shall be doing*, etc.

Bȯ	āsa̤ } karān	a̤s	āsau } karān
T̲s̲a̤	āsak } karān	tȯh^{i}	āsiv } karān
Su } Sȯ }	āsi } karān	tim } tima̤ }	āsan } karān

Future Perfect: *I*, etc., *shall have done it, he, she*, etc. (literally, *it, he, she*, etc., *will have been done by me*, etc.).

	Singular.		Plural.	
	Masc.	Fem.	Masc.	Fem.
Mė, Asi, Ta̤m^{i}, Tami, Timau	āsi kȯrmut	āsi karmat̲s̲	āsan kar-mat^{i}	āsan karma-t̲s̲a
T̲s̲ė	āset kȯrmut	āset kar-mat̲s̲	āsat kar^{i}-mat^{i}	āsat kar^{i}ma-t̲s̲a
Tȯhi	āsiva kȯr-mut	āsiva kar-mat̲s̲	āsava kar^{i}-mat^{i}	āsava kar^{i}-mat̲s̲a

IMPERATIVE MOOD.

Do thou, etc.

	SINGULAR.			PLURAL.	
	Masc. and Fem.	RESPECTFUL. Masc. and Fem.		Masc. and Fem.	RESPECTFUL. Masc. and Fem.
Tsạ	kar	kartạ, karsa, karzi, etc.	tòh[i]	kariu, kariheu	kartau, kariusa
Su } Sò }	karin	karitan	tim } timạ }	karin	karinsa

SUBJUNCTIVE MOOD.

Present: *if I do*, etc.

	SINGULAR.		PLURAL.
Bò	karahai, *or* ai karạ	ạs	karavai, *or* ai karau
Tsạ	karakai, *or* ai karak	tòh[i]	karivai, *or* ai kariv
Su } Sò }	kar[i]ai, *or* ai kari	tim } timạ }	karanai, *or* ai karan

Past (indefinite): *did I, if I did*, etc.

	SINGULAR.		PLURAL.
Bò	karahạ, *or* ai karahạ	ạs	karahau, *or* ai karahau
Tsạ	karahak, *or* ai karahak	tòh[i]	karihiu, *or* ai karihiu
Su } Sò }	karihe, *or* ai karihe	tim } timạ }	karahan, *or* ai karahan

Perfect: *I may have done*, etc. (*it*, etc., *may have been done by me*, etc.).

Mė / Asi / Tạmⁱ / Tami / Timau	āsi kȯrmut (sing. masc.)	āsi karmats (sing. fem.)
Tsė	āset kȯrmut „	āset karmats „
Tȯhi	āsiva kȯrmut „	āsiva karmats „

Pluperfect: *had I done*, or *if I had done*, etc. (*had it*, etc., *been done by me*, etc., or *if it*, etc., *had been done by me*, etc.).

Mė / Asi / Tạmⁱ / Tami / Timau	āsihe *or* ai āsihe kormut (sing. masc.)	āsihe *or* ai āsihe karmats (sing. fem.)
Tsė	āsihet *or* ai āsihet kormut „	āsihet *or* ai āsihet karmats „
Tȯhi	āsiheva *or* ai āsiheva kormut „	āsiheva *or* ai āsiheva karmats „

95. (2) Mārun, *to beat, to kill.*

Root: mār.

Infinitive: mārun, *to kill.*

Active participle: mārān, *killing.*
mārana̦, *for killing.*
mārani, *to kill.*
māranuk, *of killing.*

Conjunctive participle: mārit, *having killed.*

Adverbial participle: mārönⁱ, *on killing.*

Perfect participle: mormut, *killed.*

Nouns of agency: { māranwol, mārawun, } *a killer, one about to kill.*

INDICATIVE MOOD.

Present (continnous): *I am killing*, etc.

Singular.				Plural.			
Masc.		Fem.		Masc.		Fem.	
Bȯ chhus	mārān	bȯ chhas	mārān	ạs chhi	mārān	ạs chhė	mārān
Tsạ chhuk		tsạ chhak		tòh^{i} chhi-va		tòh^{i} chhė-vạ	
Su chhu		sọ chhė		tim chhi		timạ chhė	

Imperfect: *I was killing*, etc.

Bȯ osus	mārān	bȯ ösas	mārān	ạs ös^{i}	mārān	ạs āsa	mārān
Tsạ osuk		tsạ ösak		tòh^{i} ös^{i}va		tòh^{i} āsavạ	
Su os		sȯ ös		tim ös^{i}		timạ āsạ	

Past (indefinite): *I killed*, etc. (*it*, etc., *was killed by me*, etc.).

	Singular.		Plural.	
	Masc.	Fem.	Masc.	Fem.
Mė, Asi, Tạm^{i}, Tami, Timau	mor	mör	mör^{i}	māri
Tsė	morut	mörat	mörit	mārit
Tòhi	morva	mörva	mör^{i}va	mār^{i}va

Perfect: *I have killed*, etc. (*it*, etc., *was killed by me*, etc.).

Mė, Asi, Tạmⁱ, Tami, Timau	chhu mormut (sing. masc.)	chhė mörmạts (sing. fem.)
	chhi mörimạtⁱ (plu. masc.)	chhė mārimatsa (plu. fem.)
Tsė	chhut mormut (sing. masc.)	chhėt mormats (sing. fem.)
Tȯhi	chhuva mormut ,,	chhėva mormats ,, etc.

Pluperfect—1st form: *I*, etc., *had killed*, etc. (*he*, etc., *had been killed by me*, etc.)

	Singular.		Plural.	
	Masc.	Fem.	Masc.	Fem.
Mė, Asi, Tạmⁱ, Tami, Timau	mārov, *or* māryov, *or* māreyov	mārey, *or* māreyey	mārey, *or* māreyey	māreyi, *or* māreyeyi
Tsė	māriot, *or* māryot, *or* māreyot	māriet, *or* māreyet	māriet, *or* māreyet	māreyit
Tȯhi	māriova, *or* māreyova	māreyvạ, *or* māreyeva	māreyvạ	māreyivạ

Pluperfect—2nd form: *I had killed*, etc. (*it*, etc., *had been killed by me*, etc.).

	Singular.		Plural.	
	Masc.	Fem.	Masc.	Fem.
Mė, Asi, Tạm^{i}, Tami, Timau	os mormut	ös mörmats	ös^{i} mörimat^{i}	āsạ mārimatsa
Tsė	osut mormut	ösạt mormats	ösit mörimit^{i}	āsat mārimatsa
Tȯhi	osva mormut	ösva mormats	os^{i}va mörimit^{i}	āsava mārimatsa

Future: *I will kill*, etc.

Singular.		Plural.	
Bȯ	mārạ	ạs	mārau
Tsạ	mārak	tȯh^{i}	māriu
Su, Sȯ	māri	tim, timạ	māran

Future (continuous): *I*, etc., *shall be killing*.

Bȯ	āsạ mārān	ạs	āsau mārān
Tsạ	āsak mārān	tȯh^{i}	āsiu mārān
Su, Sȯ	āsi mārān	tim, timạ	āsan mārān

Future Perfect: *I*, etc., *shall have killed* (*he*, etc., *will have been killed by me*, etc.); used also as Subjunctive Perfect: *I*, etc., *may have been killed* (*he*, etc., *may have been killed by me*, etc.).

Mė, Asi, Tạm꞉, Tami, Timau	āsi mormut (sing. masc.)	āsi mörmats̠ (sing. fem.)
T̠sė	āset mormut „	āsėt mörmats̠ „
Tȯhi	āsiva mormut „	āsiva mörmats̠ „ etc.

IMPERATIVE MOOD.

Kill thou, do thou, etc., *kill.*

	SINGULAR.			PLURAL.	
	Masc. and Fem.	RESPECTFUL. Masc. and Fem.		Masc. and Fem.	RESPECTFUL. Masc. and Fem.
T̠sạ	mār	mārtạ, mārsa, mārzi	tȯh꞉	māriu	mārtau, māriusa
Su, Sȯ	mārin	māritan	tim, timạ	mārin	mārinsa

Subjunctive Mood.

Present: *I may kill*, or *if I kill*, etc.

Singular.		Plural.	
Bȯ	māra̩, mārahai, *or* ai māra̩	a̩s	mārau, māravai, *or* ai mārau
Tsa̩	mārak, mārakai, *or* ai mārak	tȯh^{i}	māriv, marivai, *or* ai māriv
Su, Sȯ	māri, mār^{i}ai, *or* ai mari	tim, tima̩	māran, māranai, *or* ai māran

Past (indefinite): *did I kill*, or *if I killed*, etc.

Bȯ	māraha̩, *or* ai māraha	a̩s	mārahau, *or* ai mārahau
Tsa̩	mārahak, *or* ai marahak	tȯh^{i}	mārihiu, *or* ai mārihiu
Su, Sȯ	marihe, *or* ai marihe	tim, tima̩	mārahan, *or* ai mārahan

Perfect: *I may have killed*, etc.

Mė, Asi, etc.	āsi mormut, etc., same as Future Perfect, Indicative Mood.

Pluperfect: *had I killed*, or *if I had killed*, etc.

Mė Asi Tạmi Tami Timau	āsihe, *or* ai āsihe mormut (sing. masc.)	āsihe, *or* ai āsihe mormats (sing. fem.)
Tsė	āsihet, *or* ai āsihet mormut ,,	āsihet, *or* ai āsihet mormats ,,
Tȯhi	āsiheva, *or* ai āsiheva mormut ,,	āsiheva, *or* ai āsiheva mormats ,, etc.

Causative Verbs.

96. These are formed from the simple verbs by changing the infinitive termination *-un* into *-an*, and adding *-āwun;* as, *pakun*, to go, *pakanāwun*, to cause to go; *karun*, to do, *karanāwun*, to cause to do; *ratun*, to seize, *ratanāwun*, to cause to seize; *tsaṭun*, to cut, *tsaṭanāwun*, to cause to cut; *khanun*, to dig, *khananāwun*, to cause to dig; *kheun*, to eat, *kheanāwun* or *kheāwun*, to cause to eat, to feed; *dorun*, to run, *doranāwun*, to cause to run.

97. Some verbs have a shortened causative form in use; as, *atsun*, to enter, *tsānun* (for *atsanāwun*), to cause to enter; *lagun*, to be attached or applied, *lāgun*, to cause to be attached, to attach or apply; *marun*, to die, *mārun*, to cause to die, to kill; *dazun*, to burn, *zālun*, to cause to burn; *cheun*, to drink, *cheāwun*, to cause to drink; *kheun*, to eat, *kheāwun*, to cause to eat; *phaṭun*, to break (of itself), *phāṭawun*, to cause to break; *khasun*, to ascend, *khārun*, to cause to ascend; *shongun*, to sleep, to lie down, *sāwun* or *shonganāwun*, to cause to lie down.

98. A few verbs have different words in use as causatives; thus, *woṭhun*, to rise, *woṭhanāwun* or *tulun*, to cause to rise,

to lift up; *piun*, to fall, *pāwun* or *trāwun*, to cause to fall, to throw down.

99. A causative can be treated in the same way as a simple verb, by changing the infinitive termination *-un* into *-an*, and adding *-āwun*, and thus making it into a double causative. A few such verbs are in use; as, *kheāwun*, to feed, *kheāwanāwun*, to cause one to feed another; *phāṭawun*, to break something, *phāṭanāwun*, to cause one to break something; *tulun*, to lift up, *tulanāwun*, to cause one to lift up something.

100. Examples of causative verbs—

Bachun, to escape; *bachāwun; bachāwanāwun.*

Behun, to sit down; *behanāwun; behanāwanāwun.*

Bozun, to hear, to understand; *bozanāwun; bozanāwanāwun.*

Diun, to give; *diāwun; diāwanāwun.*

Dorun, to run; *doranāwun; doranāwanāwun.*

Karun, to do; *karanāwun; karanāwanāwun.*

Marun, to die; *mārun; māranāwun.*

Piun, to fall; *pāwun; pāwanāwun.*

Passive Verbs.

101. The rule for the formation of the passive voice is most simple and regular. The termination *-un* of the infinitive is changed into *-ana*, which remains uninflected, and this is accompanied by the verb *yiun*, or *yun*, to come, inflected to agree with its nominative in person, gender, and number.

Example—

Mārun, *to kill.*

Mārana yiun, *to be killed.*

Bò chhus mārana yiwān, *I am being killed.*

Bò ās mārana yiwān, *I was killed.*

Bò yima mārana yiwān, *I shall be killed.*

INDICATIVE MOOD.

Mārana yiun, *to be killed.*

Present : *I*, etc., *am being killed.*

Bŏ chhus	mārana	yiwān,	*I* (masc.) *am being killed*
„ chhas	„	„	*I* (fem.) „ „
Tsạ chhuk	„	„	*thou* (masc.) *art being killed*
„ chhak	„	„	*thou* (fem.) „ „
Su chhu	„	„	*he is being killed*
Sŏ chhė	„	„	*she* „ „
Ạs chhi	„	„	*we* (masc.) *are being killed*
„ chhė	„	„	*we* (fem.) „ „
Tŏhĭ chhivạ	„	„	*you* (masc.) *are being killed*
„ chhėvạ	„	„	*you* (fem.) „ „
Tim chhi	„	„	*they* (masc.) *are being killed*
Timạ chhė	„	„	*they* (fem.) „ „

Imperfect : *I*, etc., *was being killed.*

Bŏ osus	mārana	yiwān,	*I* (masc.) *was being killed*
„ ösạs	„	„	*I* (fem.) „ „
etc.	etc.	etc.	

Past (indefinite) : *I*, etc., *was killed.*

Bŏ ās	mārana,	*I* (masc.) *was killed*
„ āyes	„	*I* (fem.) „
etc.	etc.	

Past Perfect : *I*, etc., *have been killed.*

Bŏ chhus āmut	mārana,	*I* (masc.) *have been killed*
„ chhas āmạts	„	*I* (fem.) „ „
etc.	etc.	etc.

Pluperfect : *I*, etc., *had been killed.*

Bŏ osus āmut	mārana,	*I* (masc.) *had been killed*
„ ösạs āmạts	„	*I* (fem.) „ „
etc.	etc.	etc.

Future: *I*, etc., *shall be killed.*

Bȯ yima mārana, *I shall be killed*
T̲s̲ạ yik „ *thou wilt be killed*
etc. etc. etc.

The above will be sufficient by way of example to show how the passive voice of verbs is formed. As the verb *yiun* alone is conjugated, the principal parts of this verb are now subjoined.

102. Yiun, *to come.*

Root: yi (ā).

Infinitive: yun, yiun, *to come.*

Present participle: yiwān, *coming.*
yinuk, *of coming.*

Conjunctive participle: yit, *having come.*

Past participle: āmut (sing. masc.), *come.*
āmat̲s̲ (sing. fem.), *come.*
āmạtⁱ (plu. masc.), *come.*
āmạt̲s̲ạ (plu. fem.), *come.*

Nouns of agency: yinawol, yinawun, } *a comer, one about to come.*

INDICATIVE MOOD.

Present (regular): *I*, etc., *am coming.*

Bȯ chhus, bȯ chhas yiwān, *I am coming*, etc.

Imperfect (regular): *I*, etc., *was coming.*

Bȯ osus, bȯ ösạs yiwān, *I was coming*, etc.

Perfect (regular): *I have come*, etc.

Bȯ chhus T̲s̲ạ chhuk Su chhu	āmut, *I have come* (sing. masc.)	bȯ chhas t̲s̲ạ chhak sȯ chhė	āmạt̲s̲, *I have come* (sing. fem.)

Pluperfect (regular): *I had come*, etc.

Bȯ osus Tsạ osuk } āmut (sing. masc.) Su os	bȯ ösạs tsạ ösạk } āmạts (sing. fem.) sȯ ös

Past Indefinite: *I*, etc., *came*.

Singular.		Plural.	
Masc.	Fem.	Masc.	Fem.
Bȯ ās	bȯ āyas	ạs āy	ạs āyi
Tsạ āk	tsạ āyak	tȯh^{i} öva	tȯh^{i} āyiva
Su āu, *or* āw	sȯ āyi	tim āy	timạ āyi

Pluperfect: *I*, etc., *had come* (used also as Subjunctive).

Bȯ āyos	bȯ āyeyas	ạs ayey	ạs āyeyi
Tsạ āyok	tsạ āyeyėk	tȯh^{i} āyevạ	tȯh^{i} āyeyiva
Su āyov, *or* ayev	sȯ āyeyi	tim āyey	timạ āyeyi

Future: *I*, etc., *will come.*

Singular.		Plural.	
Bȯ	yima	ạs	yimau
Tsạ	yik	tȯh^{i}	yiyiu
Su } Sȯ	yiyi	tim } timạ	yin

Future Continuous (regular): *I*, etc., ***shall be coming.***

Bȯ āsạ yiwān	ạs āsau yiwān

Future Perfect (regular): *I*, etc., ***shall have come.***

Bȯ āsạ āmut, bȯ āsạ āmats	ạs āsạu āmat[i], ạs āsau āma-tsa, etc.

IMPERATIVE MOOD.

Come thou, etc.

SINGULAR.		PLURAL.	
Tsạ	yi (yur[i]wala)	tȯh[i]	yiyiu
Su, Sȯ	yiyin	tim, timạ	yiyin

SUBJUNCTIVE MOOD.

Present (regular): *If I go* or *may go.*

Bȯ ai yima, etc.

Past: *did I*, etc., *go.*

SINGULAR.		PLURAL.	
Bȯ	yimahạ	ạs	yimahau
Tsạ	yihak	tȯh[i]	yiyihiu
Su, Sȯ	yiyihe	tim, timạ	yihan

PRONOMINAL AFFIXES.

103. Pronominal affixes, representing all the personal pronouns except the first person plural, are added to the various parts of the verb in each tense of each mood; and,

when thus joined to a verb, they may be the accusative, the dative, or the agentive of it.

These affixes are constantly used, and, unless they are thoroughly understood, they will always be a source of confusion. The following table and examples will help to explain them :—

104. *Pronominal Affixes joined to Verbs.*

PERSON.	SINGULAR.				PLURAL.
	Ag. for past tense of trans. verbs ("by me, thee, him, you, them").	Acc. for pres. and fut. tenses of trans. verbs.	Acc. for past tense of trans. verbs ("I, thou, he, you, they, killed, etc., by").	Dat. for all tenses ("to me, thee, him, you, them").	Ag. Acc. Dat. for all tenses.
1st	-m	-m	-s	-m	—
2nd	-t	-t (i)	-k	-i	-va
3rd	-n	-n (s)	-n	-s	-k

105. *Accusative Pronominal Affixes used with Verb in the Present Tense.*

Bò chhus mārān, *I* (masc.) *am killing*	tsė,	*thee*,	*or* bò chhusai mārān
	su, sò,	*him*, *her*,	„ „ chhusan „
	tòh^{i},	*you*,	„ „ chhusava „
	tim, timạ,	*them*,	„ „ chhusak „
Bò chhas mārān, *I* (fem.) *am killing*	tsė,	*thee*,	*or* bò chhasai mārān
	su, sò,	*him*, *her*,	„ „ chhasan „
	tòh^{i},	*you*,	„ „ chhasava „
	tim, timạ,	*them*,	„ „ chhasak „

Tsạ chhuk mārān, *thou* (masc.) *art killing*	mė,	*me*,	*or* tsạ chhuham mārān
	su, sȯ,	*him*, *her*,	,, ,, chhuhan ,,
	tim, timạ,	*them*,	,, ,, chhuhak ,,

Tsạ chhak mārān, *thou* (fem.) *art killing*	mė,	*me*,	*or* tsạ chhaham mārān
	su, sȯ,	*him*, *her*,	,, ,, chhahan ,,
	tim, timạ,	*them*,	,, ,, chhahak ,,

Su chhu mārān, *he is killing*	mė,	*me*,	*or* su chhum mārān
	tsė,	*thee*,	,, ,, chhui ,,
	su, sȯ,	*him*, *her*,	,, ,, chhun ,,
	tȯh^{i},	*you*,	,, ,, chhuva ,,
	tim, timạ,	*them*,	,, ,, chhuk ,,

Sȯ chhė mārān, *she is killing*	mė,	*me*,	*or* sȯ chhėm mārān
	tsė,	*thee*,	,, ,, chhei ,,
	su, sȯ,	*him*, *her*,	,, ,, chhėn ,,
	tȯh^{i},	*you*,	,, ,, chhėva ,,
	tim, timạ,	*them*,	,, ,, chhėk ,,

Ạs chhi mārān, *we* (masc.) *are killing*	tsė,	*thee*,	*or* ạs chhī mārān tsạ
	su, sȯ,	*him*, *her*,	,, ,, chhin ,,
	tȯh^{i},	*you*,	,, ,, chhiva ,,
	tim, timạ,	*them*,	,, ,, chhik ,,

Ạs chhė mārān, *we* (fem.) *are killing*	tsė,	*thee*,	*or* ạs chhei mārān
	su,	*him*,	„ „ chhėn „
	sȯ,	*her*,	„ „ chhėn „
	tȯh^{i},	*you*,	„ „ chhėva „
	tim,	*them*,	„ „ chhėk „
	timạ,	*them*,	„ „ chhėk „

Tȯh^{i} chhiva mārān, *you* (masc.) *are killing*	mė,	*me*,	*or* tȯh^{i} chhivom mārān
	su,	*him*,	„ „ chhivon „
	sȯ,	*her*,	„ „ chhivon „
	tim,	*them*,	„ „ chhivok „
	timạ,	*them*,	„ „ chhivok „

Tȯh^{i} chhėvạ mārān, *you* (fem.) *are killing*	mė,	*me*,	*or* tȯh^{i} chhėvom mārān
	su,	*him*,	„ „ chhėvon „
	sȯ,	*her*,	„ „ chhėvon „
	tim,	*them*,	„ „ chhėvok „
	timạ,	*them*,	„ „ chhėvok „

Tim chhi mārān, *they* (masc.) *are killing*	mė,	*me*,	*or* tim chhim mārān
	tsė,	*thee*,	„ „ chhī „
	su,	*him*,	„ „ chhin „
	sȯ,	*her*,	„ „ chhin „
	tȯh^{i},	*you*,	„ „ chhiva „
	tim,	*them*,	„ „ chhik „
	timạ,	*them*,	„ „ chhik „

Timạ chhė mārān, *they* (fem.) *are killing*	mė,	*me*,	*or* timạ chhėm mārān
	tse,	*thee*,	„ „ chhėt „
	su,	*him*,	„ „ chhėn „
	sȯ,	*her*,	„ „ chhėn „
	tȯh^{i},	*you*,	„ „ chhėva „
	tim,	*them*,	„ „ chhėk „
	timạ,	*them*,	„ „ chhėk „

106. *Dative Pronominal Affixes used with Verb in the Present Tense.*

Bò chhus diwān, *I* (masc.) *am giving*	tsė,	*to thee,*	*or* bò chhusai diwān
	tas,	,, *him, her,* etc.,	,, ,, chhusas ,,
	tòhi,	,, *you,*	,, ,, chhusava ,,
	timan,	,, *them,*	,, ,, chhusak ,,

Bò chhas diwān, *I* (fem.) *am giving*	tsė,	*to thee,*	*or* bò chhasai diwān
	tas,	,, *him,* etc.,	,, ,, chhasas ,,
	tòhi,	,, *you,*	,, ,, chhasava ,,
	timan,	,, *them,*	,, ,, chhasak ,,

Tsạ chhuk diwān, *thou* (masc.) *art giving*	mė,	*to me,*	*or* tsạ chhuham diwān
	tas,	,, *him,* etc.,	,, ,, chhuhas ,,
	timan,	,, *them,*	,, ,, chhuhak ,,

Tsạ chhak diwān, *thou* (fem.) *art giving*	mė,	*to me,*	*or* tsạ chhaham diwān
	tas,	,, *him,* etc.,	,, ,, chhahas ,,
	timan,	,, *them,*	,, ,, chhahak ,,

Su chhu diwān, *he is giving*	mė,	*to me,*	*or* su chhum diwān
	tsė,	,, *thee,*	,, ,, chhui ,,
	tas,	,, *him,* etc.,	,, ,, chhus ,,
	tòhi,	,, *you,*	,, ,, chhuva ,,
	timan,	,, *them,*	,, ,, chhuk ,,

Sò chhė diwān, *she is giving*	mė,	*to me,*	*or* sò chhėm diwān
	tsė,	,, *thee,*	,, ,, chhei ,,
	tas,	,, *him,* etc.,	,, ,, chhės ,,
	tòhi,	,, *you,*	,, ,, chhėva ,,
	timan,	,, *them,*	,, ,, chhėk ,,

Ạs chhi diwān, *we* (masc.) *are giving*	tsė,	*to thee,*	*or* ạs chhī diwān
	tas,	,, *him,* etc.,	,, ,, chhịs ,,
	tòhi,	,, *you,*	,, ,, chhịva ,,
	timan,	,, *them,*	,, ,, chhik ,,

Ạs chhė diwān, *we* (fem.) *are giving*	tsė,	*to thee,*	*or* ạs chhei diwān
	tas,	„ *him*, etc.,	„ „ chhės „
	tòhi,	„ *you,*	„ „ chhėva „
	timan,	„ *them,*	„ „ chhėk „
Tòh^{i} chhiva diwān, *you* (masc.) *are giving*	mė,	*to me,*	*or* tòh^{i} chhivom diwān
	tas,	„ *him*, etc.,	„ „ chhivos „
	timan,	„ *them,*	„ „ chhivok „
Tòh^{i} chhėva diwān, *you* (fem.) *are giving*	mė,	*to me,*	*or* tòh^{i} chhevom diwān
	tas,	„ *him*, etc.,	„ „ chhevos „
	timan,	„ *them,*	„ „ chhevok „
Tim chhi diwān, *they* (masc.) *are giving*	mė,	*to me,*	*or* tim chhum diwān
	tsė,	„ *thee,*	„ „ chhī „
	tas,	„ *him*, etc.,	„ „ chhis „
	tòhi,	„ *you,*	„ „ chhiva „
	timan,	„ *them,*	„ „ chhik „
Timạ chhė diwān, *they* (fem.) *are giving*	mė,	*to me,*	*or* timạ chhėm diwān
	tsė,	„ *thee,*	„ „ chhei „
	tas,	„ *him*, etc.,	„ „ chhės „
	tòhi,	„ *you,*	„ „ chhėva „
	timan,	„ *them,*	„ „ chhėk „

107. *Accusative Pronominal Affixes used with Verb in the Future Tense.*

Bò mārạ, *I will kill*	tsė,	*thee,*	*or* bò mārat (tsạ),	*or simply* mārat
	su, *him,* / sò, *her,*		„ „ māran,	„ māran
	tòh^{i},	*you,*	„ „ mārava,	„ mārava
	tim, / timạ,	*them,*	„ „ mārak,	„ mārak
Tsạ mārak, *thou wilt kill*	mė,	*me,*	*or* tsạ mārạham,	*or simply* mārạham
	su, *him,* / sò, *her,*		„ „ mārạhan,	„ mārạhan
	tim, / timạ,	*them,*	„ „ mārạhak,	„ mārạhak

Su *or* sò māri *he or she will kill*	mė,	*me*,	*or* su māriam,	*or simply* māriam
	tsė,	*thee*,	„ „ mārī (tsė),	„ mārī
	su, sò,	*him, her,*	„ „ mārias,	„ mārias
	tòh^i,	*you*,	„ „ māriva,	„ māriva
	tim, timạ,	*them*,	„ „ māriak,	„ māriak

Ạs mārau, *we will kill*	tsė,	*thee*,	*or* ạs mārot (tsạ),	*or simply* mārot
	su, sò,	*him, her,*	„ „ māron,	„ māron
	tòh^i,	*you*,	„ „ mārova,	„ mārova
	tim, timạ,	*them*,	„ „ mārok,	„ mārok

Tòh^i māriu, *you will kill*	mė	*me*,	*or* tòh^i māriom,	*or simply* māriom
	su, sò,	*him, her,*	„ „ mārion,	„ mārion
	tim, timạ,	*them*,	„ „ māriok,	„ māriok

Tim *or* timạ māran, *they* (masc. or fem.) *will kill*	mė,	*me*,	*or* tim māranam,	*or simply* māranam
	tsė,	*thee*,	„ „ māranai(tsėh),	„ māranai
	su, sò,	*him, her,*	„ „ māranas,	„ māranas
	tòh^i,	*you*,	„ „ māranava,	„ māranava
	tim, timạ,	*them*,	„ „ māranak,	„ māranak

108. *Dative Pronominal Affixes used with Verb in the Future Tense.*

Bò dapạ, *I will speak*	tsė,	*to thee*,	*or* bò dapai,	*or simply* dapai
	tas,	„ *him*, etc.,	„ dapas,	„ dapas
	tòhi,	„ *you*,	„ „ dapova,	„ dapova
	timan,	„ *them*,	„ „ dapak,	„ dapak

Tsa̱ dapak, *thou wilt speak*	mė,	*to me*	*or* tsa̱	dapaham,	*or simply*	dapaham
	tas,	„ *him*, etc.,	„	dapahas,	„	dapahas
	timan,	„ *them*,	„ „	dapahak,	„	dapahak

Su *or* sȯ dapi, *he* or *she will speak*	mė,	*to me*,	*or* su	dapiam,	*or simply*	dapiam
	tse,	„ *thee*,	„ „	dapī,	„	dapī
	tas,	„ *him*, etc.,	„	dapias,	„	dapias
	tȯhi,	„ *you*,	„ „	dapiva,	„	dapiva
	timan,	„ *them*,	„ „	dapiak, dapek,	„	dapiak

A̤s dapau, *we will speak*	tsė,	*to thee*,	*or* a̤s	dapoī,	*or simply*	dapoī
	tas,	„ *him*, etc.,	„	dapos,	„	dapos
	tȯhi,	„ *you*,	„ „	dapova,	„	dapova
	timan,	„ *them*,	„ „	dapok,	„	dapok

Tȯhⁱ dapiu, *you will speak*	mė,	*to me*,	*or* tȯhⁱ	dapiom,	*or simply*	dapiom
	tas,	„ *him*, etc.,	„	dapios,	„	dapios
	timan,	„ *them*,	„ „	dapiok	„	dapiok

Tim *or* tima dapan, *they* (masc. or fem.) *will speak*	mė,	*to me*,	*or* tim	dapanam,	*or simply*	dapanham
	tsė,	„ *thee*,	„ „	dapanai,	„	dapanai
	tas,	„ *him*, etc.,	„	dapanas,	„	dapanas
	tȯhi,	„ *you*,	„ „	dapanava,	„	dapanava
	timan,	„ *them*,	„ „	dapanak	„	dapanak

109. *Agentive Pronominal Affixes used with Verb in the Past Tense.*

Mor, or more properly *morᵘ*, is the past indef. 3rd pers. masc. sing. of *mārun*, to kill. ***Mė mor su***, or simply *morum*, he was killed by me; or, as we should say in English, "I killed him."

From morᵘ (past indef. masc. sing.), ***killed***	morum,	*he was killed by me*,	or	*I killed him*
	morut,	„ „ „ *thee*,	„	*thou killedst him*
	morun,	„ „ „ *him*,	„	*he killed him*
	moruva,	„ „ „ *you*,	„	*you killed him*
	moruk,	„ „ „ *them*,	„	*they killed him*

From mör (past indef. fem. sing.), *killed*	möram,	*she was killed by me,*	or *I killed her*
	mörat,	„ „ „ *thee,*	„ *thou killedst her*
	möran,	„ „ „ *him,*	„ *he killed her*
	mörava,	„ „ „ *you,*	„ *you killed her*
	mörak,	„ „ „ *them,*	„ *they killed her*
From mör^{i} (past indef. masc. plu.), *killed*	mörim,	*they were killed by me,*	or *I killed them*
	mörit,	„ „ „ *thee,*	„ *thou killedst them*
	mörin,	„ „ „ *him,*	„ *he killed them*
	möriva,	„ „ „ *you,*	„ *you killed them*
	mörik,	„ „ „ *them,*	„ *they killed them*
From māri (past indef. fem. plu.), *killed*	mārim,	*they were killed by me,*	or *I killed them*
	mārit,	„ „ „ *thee,*	„ *thou killedst them*
	mārin,	„ „ „ *him,*	„ *he killed them*
	māriva,	„ „ „ *you,*	„ *you killed them*
	mārik,	„ „ „ *them,*	„ *they killed them*

110. *Accusative Pronominal Affixes used with Transitive Verbs in the Past Tense.*

Mor^{u} is the masculine singular, neither the agent nor the object being definitely stated.

Morun is "he or it (masc. sing.) killed." Here the *n* represents the agent; but all that can be known about the object beaten or killed is that it is the masculine singular; *moranas* is "he, it, killed by me;" or, more literally, "I was killed by him or it."

From morum, *I killed* (masc. sing.)	mormak, *I killed thee,* literally,	*thou wast killed by me*
„ mörim (masc. plu.)	mörimava, „ *you,* „	*you were killed by me*
	mörimak, „ *them,* „	*they were killed by me*

From mārim (fem. plu.)	mārimak, *I killed them*, literally, *they were killed by me*
From morut, *thou killedst*	mortas, *thou killedst me*, literally, *I was killed by thee*
	mortan, „ *him*, „ *he was killed by thee*
„ mörit (masc. plu.)	mör¹tak, „ *them*, „ *they were killed by thee*
„ mārit (fem. plu.)	māritak, „ *them*, „ *they were killed by thee*
From morun, *he killed* (masc. sing.)	moranas, *he killed me*, literally, *I was killed by him*
	moranak, „ *thee*, „ *thou wast killed by him*
„ mörin (masc. plu.)	mörinava, „ *you*, „ *you were killed by him*
From moruva, *you killed* (masc. sing.)	moravas, *you killed me*, literally, *I was killed by you*
	moravan, „ *him*, „ *he was killed by you*
„ möriva (masc. plu.)	mörivak, „ *them*, „ *they were killed by you*
„ māriva (fem. plu.)	mārivak, „ *them*, „ *they were killed by you*
From moruk, *they killed* (masc. sing.)	morhas, *they killed me*, literally, *I was killed by them*
	morhak, „ *thee*, „ *thou wast killed by them*
„ mörak (fem. sing.)	mörhas, „ *me*, „ *I was killed by them*
	mörhak, „ *thee*, „ *thou wast killed by them*

From mörik (masc. plu.)	mörihava, *they killed you*, literally, *you were killed by them*
„ märik (fem. plu.)	märihava, „ *you*, „ *you were killed by them*

111. *Dative Pronominal Affixes used with Verb in the Past Tense.*

From dòpum, *I spoke* (acc. masc. sing., *was spoken by me*)	dòpmai, *I spoke to thee*
	dòpmas, „ „ *him* or *her*
	dòpmava, „ „ *you*
	dòpmak, „ „ *them*
From dòput, *thou spakest* (acc. masc. sing.)	dòptam, *thou spakest to me*
	dòptas, „ „ *him*
	dòptak, „ „ *them*
From dòpun, *he spoke* (acc. masc. sing.)	dòpnam, *he spoke to me*
	dòpnai, „ „ *thee*
	dòpnas, „ „ *him*
	dòpnava, „ „ *you*
	dòpnak, „ „ *them*
From dòpuva, *you spoke* (acc. masc. sing.)	dòpvom, *you spoke to me*
	dòpvas, „ „ *him*
	dòpvak, „ „ *them*
From dopuk, *they spoke* (acc. masc. sing.)	dopham, *they spoke to me*
	dophai, „ „ *thee*
	dophas, „ „ *him*
	dophava, „ „ *you*
	dophak, „ „ *them*

112. When the past participle is used with the auxiliary verb "to be," the participle agrees in number and gender with the accusative, but the affix is added only to the auxiliary verb; as—

Mè chhu vuchhmut [he, it (masc. sing.), is seen by me], I

have seen him; or, *mė chhum vuchhmut*, or simply, *vuchhmut chhum.*

Mė chhė vuchhmats [she (fem. sing.) has been seen by me], I have seen her; or, *mė chhėm vuchhmats*, or simply, *vuchhmats chhėm.*

Tsė chhut vuchhmut, thou hast seen him; or, *vuchhmut chhut.*

Tsė chhėt vuchhmats, thou hast seen her; or, *vuchhmats chhėt.*

Tôhi chhuva vuchhmut, you have seen him; or, *vuchhmut chhuva.*

Tôhi chhėvạ vuchhmats, you have seen her; or, *vuchhmats chhĕva.*

Tạm^{i} *chhu vuchhmut*, he has seen him (acc. masc. sing.); or, *vuchhmut chhun.*

Tạm^{i} *chhė vuchhmats*, he has seen her (acc. fem. sing.): or, *vuchhmats chhėn.*

Timau chhu vuchhmut, they have seen him (acc. masc. sing.); or, *vuchhmut chhuk.*

Timau chhė vuchhmats, they have seen her (acc. fem. sing.); or, *vuchhmats chhek.*

Mė os vuchhmut, I had seen him (acc. masc. sing.); or, *vuchhmut osum.*

Mė ös vuchhmats, I had seen her (acc. fem. sing.) or, *vuchhmats ösam.*

Tạm^{i} *os vuchhmut*, he had seen him (acc. masc. sing.); or, *vuchhmut osun.*

Tạm^{i} *ös vuchhmats*, he had seen her (acc. fem. sing.); or, *vuchhmats ösan.*

Tami os vuchhmut, she had seen him (acc. masc. sing.); or, *vuchhmut ösun.*

Tami ös vuchhmats, she had seen her (acc. fem. sing.); or, *vuchhmats ösan.*

Timau os vuchhmut, they had seen him (acc. masc. sing.); or, *vuchhmut osuk.*

Timau ös vuchhmats, they had seen her (acc. fem. sing.); or, *vuchhmats ösak.*

Mė āsi vuchhmut, I may have seen him (acc. masc. sing.); or, *vuchhmut āsem.*

Mė āsi vuchhmats, I may have seen her (acc. fem. sing.); or, *vuchhmats āsem.*

Tạm^{i} *āsi vuchhmut*, he may have seen him (acc. masc. sing.); or, *vuchhmut āsen.*

Tạm^{i} *āsi vuchhmats*, he may have seen her (acc. fem. sing.); or, *vuchhmats āsen.*

Tami āsi vuchhmut, she may have seen him (acc. masc. sing.); or, *vuchhmut āsen.*

Tami āsi vuchhmats, she may have seen her (acc. fem. sing.); or, *vuchhmats āsen.*

Timau āsi vuchhmut, they may have seen him (acc. masc. sing.); or, *vuchhmut āsek.*

Timau āsi vuchhmats, they may have seen her (acc. fem. sing.); or, *vuchhmats āsek.*

Mė ai āsihe vuchhmut, if I had seen him (acc. masc. sing.); or, *vuchhmut ai āsihem.*

Mė ai āsihe vuchhmats, if I had seen her (acc. fem. sing.); or, *vuchhmats āsihem.*

Tạm^{i} *ai āsihe vuchhmut*, as if he had seen him (acc. masc. sing.); or, *vuchhmut ai āsihen.*

Tạm^{i} *ai āsihe vuchhmats*, if he had seen her (acc. fem. sing.); or, *vuchhmats āsihen.*

Tami ai āsihe vuchhmut, if she had seen him (acc. masc. sing.); or, *vuchhmut āsihen.*

Tami ai āsihe vuchhmats, if she had seen her (acc. fem. sing.); or, *vuchhmats āsihen.*

Timau ai āsihe vuchhmut, if they had seen him (acc. masc. sing.); or, *vuchhmut āsihek.*

Timau ai āsihe vuchhmats, if they had seen her (acc. fem. sing.); or, *vuchhmats āsihek.*

113. *Observations on the above Pronominal Affixes.*

(1) The verb in the present, imperfect, and future tenses agrees with the nominative in number and gender; and the pronominal affix is either its accusative or dative; as, ***suh chhum mārān***, he is killing me; ***suh osum māran***, he was killing me; ***suh māram***, he will kill me.

(2) The past tense of transitive verbs agrees with the pronoun that would be in the objective in English, in number and gender; and, if there is only one pronominal affix, it represents the agent; and, if there are two, the first represents the agent, and the second the accusative or dative; as, ***tąmi mor***, he killed,—the verb is masc. sing.; ***tąmi mor suh***, he killed him, or ***morun suh; timau mor suh***, or ***moruk suh***, they killed him; ***tąmi mor bŏh***, or ***morun bŏh***, or ***moranas***, he killed me; ***tąmi dŏp mėh***, or ***dŏpun mėh***, or ***dŏpanam***, he said to me.

(3) In the second person singular of the future tense the *t*, and in the third person plural of the past tense the affix *-k*, are changed into *h* before an accusative or dative pronominal affix; as, ***t̠są mārat suh***, with affix, becomes, not ***māratan***, but ***mārahan; timau dŏp mėh*** becomes ***dŏpuk mėh***, and then not ***dŏpakam***, but ***dŏpaham***, or ***dŏpham***.

(4) The agentive *t* of the second person singular and *va* of the second person plural of the past tense are inseparable from the verb, whether the personal pronoun is used or not for the agent. We can say, ***mėh mor suh*** or ***morum suh, timau mor suh*** or ***moruk suh;*** but we cannot say, ***t̠sė mor suh*** or ***tŏhi mor suh***, but ***t̠sė morut suh*** or ***morut suh, tŏhi moruva suh*** or ***moruva suh***.

(5) In the third person singular and plural of transitive verbs in the future the accusative affixes for the second and third persons singular are the same as those for the dative, whereas we should have expected *t* and *n* respectively.

(6) The masculine singular of the verb in the past inde-

finite really ends in a very short *u* sound; as, *mor*^{u}, *dôp*^{u}; and hence with the affixes we have *morun*, *dòpun*; *morut*, *moruk*. When a second affix is added this *u* is either changed into *a* or disappears; as, *moranas* or *mornas*, *moratas* or *mortas*; *dòpanam* or *dòpnam*, etc.

114. The verb "to be," with the dative pronominal affixes, is constantly used to denote possession, meaning "I have," etc., thus—

Present.

Suh chhu mêh, etc., *or* suh (masc. sing.)	chhum,	*is to me*,	meaning	*I have*	*him, it*
	chhuī,	„ *thee*,	„	*thou hast*	„
	chhus,	„ *him, her*	„	*he has*	„
	chhuva,	„ *you*,	„	*you have*	„
	chhuk,	„ *them*,	„	*they have*	„

In the same manner—

Sò chhêm, she is to me, I have her, etc.

Tim chhim, they are to me, I have them, etc.

Timạ chhêm, they (fem.) are to me, I have them (fem.), etc.

Past.

Suh os mêh, etc., *or* suh (masc. sing.)	osum,	*was to me*,	meaning	*I had*	*him*, etc.
	osuī,	„ *thee*,	„	*thou hadst*	„
	osus,	„ *him*,	„	*he had*	„
	osuva,	„ *you*,	„	*you had*	„
	osuk,	„ *them*,	„	*they had*	„

In the same manner—

Sòh ös mêh, or *sòh ösạm*, she was to me, I had her.

Tim ös' mèh, or *tim ösim*, they (masc. plu.) were to me, I had them.

Timą āsą mèh, or *timą āsąm*, they (fem. plu.) were to me, I had them.

Future.

Suh āsi mèh, *or* suh	āsiam,	*will be to me*,	meaning	*I shall have him*, etc.		
	āsi *or* āsī,	„	*thee*,	„	*thou wilt*	„
	āsias *or* āsies,	„	*him*,	„	*he will*	„
	āsiava *or* āsiva,	„	*you*,	„	*you will*	„
	āsiak *or* āsok,	„	*them*,	„	*they will*	„

In the same manner—

Tim āsan mèh, or *tim āsanam*, they will be to me, I shall have them, etc.

Tim āsan tas, or *tim āsanas*, they will be to him, he will have them, etc.

Compound Verbs.

115. These may be divided into (1) those in which the verb expressing the main idea of the compound is joined to another verb; and (2) those in which it is joined to a noun or adjective.

116. *Compounds formed with the Past Conjunctive Participle.*

(1) *Intensives.* Formed by adding another verb to the past conjunctive participle of what is often the principal verb: *kaḍun*, to cast out; *kaḍit tshunun*, to cast out altogether; *mė tshun mārit suh*, I killed him outright (compare *nikālna* and *nikāldena*; and *mārna* and *mār dālna*, in Urdu).

Phīrit yiun, to return, to come back; *phīrit hèun*, to take back; *phīrit gatshun*, to go back, to return.

(2) *Potentials*. *Hèkun*, to be able; *hèkun karit*, to be able to do; *Bô chhus yih köm hèkān karit*, I am able to do this work; *Su chhu hèkān wanit*, He is able to speak.

117. There are other forms which, though not strictly compound verbs, yet are so closely allied to them that we give them here—

Statisticals. These are formed by adding a very short *ⁱ* to the root of the verb; thus, *Wanⁱ wanⁱ chhu gatshān*, He goes on his way weeping; *Khèⁱ khèⁱ su gau viòṭh*, Going on eating, he grew fat.

The present participle may be used in this way; as, *Su chhu gatshān wadān wadān*, He is going away weeping.

118. *Verbs used with another Verb in the Infinitive.*

(1) *Inceptives*. *Heun*, to take up, begin; *heun karun*, to begin to do; *Tąmⁱ hiut* (or *hyut*) *khat lèkhun*, He began to write a letter.

(2) *Desideratives*. *Yatshun*, to desire or wish; *yatshun karun*, to desire to do; *Bô chhus yatshān yih khat lèkhun*, I desire to write this letter.

(3) *Potentials*. *Tagun*, to be able, to have power; *tagun karun*, to be able to do; *Mèh tagiam nạ gharạ banāwun*, I shall not be able (or, have the power) to build a house. *Banun*, to become, to be made; *banun karun*, to be able to do; *Mè chhu nạ banān parun*, I cannot read.

119. *Impersonal Verbs.*

The third masculine singular future of *gatshun*, to go, is constantly used as an impersonal verb, meaning "ought," "it is necessary;" *gatshi karun*, ought to do; *Nechivis gatshi hechun panun sabaq*, A son ought to learn his lesson. *Pazi* and *shobi*, it is proper, from *pazun* and *shobun*, are also used as impersonals; *pazi karun*, or *shobi karun*, it is proper to do; *Tsė pazi nạ apoz wanun*, It will not be proper to thee to tell an untruth; *Kāṇsi shobi nạ apoz wanun*, It will not be proper to any one to tell an untruth, or, No one should tell a lie.

Pėun, to happen, to fall, is also used with the infinitive; *pėun karun*, to happen to do; *Tamis pėon khat lekhun*, It happened to him to write a letter, or, He happened to write a letter.

120. *Verbs used with the Inflected Infinitive.*

(1) *Lagun*, to begin, to apply one's self to; *lagun karani*, to begin to do; *Paga lagạ yih köm karani*, To-morrow I shall begin to do this work.

(2) The form *karanạ karān* implies a condition or difficulty, "he does, but . . .;" *Su chhu karanạ karān magar wadi wadi*, He works indeed, but he does it weeping.

NOMINALS.

121. These are formed by annexing a verb to an uninflected noun or adjective. The verbs mostly used for this purpose are *karun*, to do; *diun*, to give; *yiun*, to come; *khėun*, to eat; *heun*, to take; *gatshun*, to go; and they may be joined to almost any noun or adjective in the language. The infinitive agrees in gender with its noun.

Examples—

Gāsa khėun, to eat grass, graze.
Hoshyār gatshun, to become clever, awake.
Hukm diun, to command, order.
Hukm karun, to convict, sentence, command.
Kāmirust karun, to dismiss.
Kāwa diun, to give ear, listen.

Mushik hèun, to smell.
Nād diun, to call.
Shrūts karun, to clean.
T̲sòpa karaṇⁱ, to keep silent, be quiet.
Wāṭh sapadun, to cling.
Wòsh kadun, to sigh.
Yād yiun, to remember.
Zulm karun, to oppress.
Zuṭh karun, to extend.

FORMATION OF TENSES.

122. As already remarked at the beginning of Chapter V., most of the verbs in Kashmīrī are very regular. The only changes of vowels and consonants likely to cause any difficulty are those that are made for the past indefinite and pluperfect tenses; but the following simple rules will assist the student to understand these:—

1. *Changes of Vowels.*

123. Examples—

VOWEL-CHANGES.	INFINITIVE.	PAST INDEFINITE.	PAST PARTICIPLE.
ā becomes *o*	mārun, *to kill*	mor	mormut
	gālun, *to melt*	gol	golmut
	t̲sāndun, *to search*	t̲sond	t̲sondmut
	mānun, *to obey*	mon	monmut
	mānḍun, *to knead*	monḍ	monḍmut
	t̲sāpun, *to bite, chew*	t̲sop	t̲sopmut

VOWEL-CHANGES.	INFINITIVE.	PAST INDEFINITE.	PAST PARTICIPLE.
	lāgun, *to plough, attach*	log	logmut
	lāyun, *to beat*	loy (*or* loe)	loymut
	t͟sārun, *to gather*	t͟sor	t͟sormut
	wātun, *to arrive*	wot	wotmut
	kāsun, *to shave*	kos	kosmut
a becomes *ȯ*	pakun, *to go*	pȯk	pȯkmut
	malun, *to rub*	mȯl	mȯlmut
	chhalun, *to wash*	chhȯl	chhȯlmut
	marun, *to die*	mȯr	mȯrmut
	karun, *to do*	kȯr	kȯrmut
	katun, *to spin*	kȯt	kȯtmut
	khasun, *to ascend*	khȯt	khȯtmut
	manḍun, *to trample*	mȯnḍ	mȯnḍmut
	raṭun, *to take*	rȯṭ	rȯṭmut
	t͟salun, *to run away*	t͟sȯl	t͟sȯlmut
	wanun, *to speak*	wȯn	wȯnmut
	wadun, *to weep*	wȯd	wȯdmut
	walun, *to dress one's self*	wȯl	wȯlmut
	waṭun, *to close*	wȯṭ	wȯṭmut
e becomes *ū* or *yū*	sherun, *to adorn*	shūr, shyūr	shūrmut, shyūrmut
	pherun, *to turn*	phūr	phūrmut
	menun, *to measure*	myūr	myūrmut
	nerun, *to go out*	drāw, nyūr	drāmut, nyūrmut
	melun, *to meet*	myūr	myūrmut

Vowel-Changes.	Infinitive.	Past Indefinite.	Past Participle.
ė becomes *u* or *yu*	hėkun, *to be able*	hyuk	hyukmut
	lėkhun, *to write*	lyukh	lyukhmut
	thėkun, *to boast*	thyuk	thyukmut
	tsėṭun, *to crush*	tsyuṭ	tsyuṭmut
	vyėndun, *to practise*	vyund	vyundmut
	vėtsun, *to be contained*	vyuts	vyutsmut
	lėwun, *to lick*	lyu	lyumut
	nėtun, *to shear*	nyut	nyutmut
	hėun, *to take*	hyut	hyutmut
o becomes *ū*	bozun, *to hear*	būz	būzmut
	losun, *to be tired*	lūs	lūsmut
	sozun, *to send*	sūz	sūzmut
	roshun, *to be angry*	rūsh	rūshmut
	khotsun, *to fear*	khūts	khutsmut
	poshun, *to prevail*	pūsh	pushmut
	rozun, *to remain*	rūd	rudmut
ȯ becomes *u* or remains *ȯ*	phȯkun, *to blow*	phuk	phukmut
	wȯthun, *to rise*	wuth	wuthmut
	mȯngun, *to ask*	mȯng	mȯngmut
	shȯngun, *to sleep*	shȯng	shȯngmut
ī becomes *ū*	chīrun, *to squeeze*	chūr	chūrmut
	zīlun, *to shave, scrape*	zūl	zūlmut
i becomes *yu*	bihun, *to sit*	byut	byutmut
	gindun, *to play*	gyund	gyundmut
	pihun, *to grind*	pyuh	pyuhmut
	diun, *to give*	dyut	dyutmut

VOWEL-CHANGES.	INFINITIVE.	PAST INDEFINITE.	PAST PARTICIPLE.
ū remains *ū*	lūṭun, *to rob*	lūṭ	lūṭmut
	būzun, *to roast*	būz	būzmut
	lūrun, *to throw down*	lūr	lūrmut
u remains *u*	pushurun, pusharun, } *to entrust*	pushur	pushurmut
	wuchhun, *to see*	wuchh	wuchhmut
	tulun, *to lift up*	tul	tulmut

2. *Changes of Consonants.*

124. Examples—

CONSONANT-CHANGES.	INFINITIVE.	PLUPERFECT (3rd Pers. Masc. Sing.).
d becomes *z*	ladun, *to load*	lazov, *or* lazeyov
g, *l* } become *j*	mongun, *to ask*	monjov, *or* monjeyov
	shôngun, *to lie down*	shônjov
	salun, *to flee*	sajov, *or* sajeyov
	chalun, *to wash*	chajov, *or* chajeyov
k, *ṭ*, *h* } become *ch*	pakun, *to walk*	pachov, *or* pacheyov
	lekhun, *to write*	lechhov
	khaṭun, *to conceal*	khachov, *or* khacheyov
	phaṭun, *to split, sink*	phachov, *or* phacheyov
	waṭun, *to close*	wachov
	behun, *to sit*	bechov
s, *t* } become *ts*, *s*	khasun, *to ascend*	khatsov, *or* khatseyov
	losun, *to be tired*	losov, *or* losyov
	wātun, *to arrive*	wātsov, *or* wātseyov

125. **Irregular Verbs.**

Infinitive.	Present Participle.	Future 1st Pers. Sing.	Conjunct. Part.	Past Indefinite 3rd Pers. Masc. Sing.	Past Participle.	Pluperfect.
1. Āsun, *to be*	āsān	āsạ	āsit	os	osmut	āseyov
2. *Chėun, *to drink*	chėwān	*chėmạ	chėt	chaw	chaumut	cheyov
3. Diun, *or* dyun, *to give*	diwān	dimạ	dit	diut, *or* dyut	diutmut, *or* dyutmut	ditsov
4. Hėun, *to take*	hėwān	hėmạ	hėt	hiuk, *or* hyuk	hiukmut, *or* hyukmut	hėt<u>s</u>ov
5. Khėun, *to eat*	khėwān	khėmạ	khėt	khėāw	khėomut	khėyov
6. Marun, *to die*	marān	marạ	marit	mud	modmut	maryov
7. Niun, *to take*	niwān	nimạ	nit	niu	niumut, *or* nyumut	niyov
8. Nerun, *to go out*	newān	nerạ	nerit	drāw	drāmut	drāyov
9. Pėun, *to fall*	pėwān	pėmạ	pėt	pėāw	pėomut	pėyov
10. Yun, *or* yiun, *to come*	yiwān	yimạ	yit	āw	āmut	āyov

* It will be observed that when a root ends in a vowel, the future first person singular has the letter *m* inserted before the *a*; as, *karun*, to do; *kar*; *karạ*, I will do: *chėun*, to drink; *chė*; *chėmạ*, I will drink.

CHAPTER VI.

INDECLINABLE WORDS.

1. Adverbs.

126. The following table will show the connection between a quintuple series of adverbs, and adjective pronouns used as adverbs, with the demonstrative, interrogative, and relative pronouns. The personal pronoun *suh* is often used as the correlative of the relative pronoun *yus*.

Of the words in the table those in the columns of Time and Place are proper adverbs, and are indeclinable; but their number can be increased and their meanings modified by such terminations as *-ām*, *-tām*, *-tāmat*, *-ān*, meaning generally "till," "up to;" as, *yotām*, *kotām*, *kotāmat; yorām*, *yotān*, *yutān*. *Yot* and *yor*, etc., with their affixes, are also used for time; *yutān* meaning "until," "as long as," etc. Other affixes are *-a*, *-i*, *-it*, *-ut*, *-ai*, *-oi*, *-ui*, which generally intensify the meanings; as, *kut dur*, or *kota dur*, how far; *yati*, *yeti*, *yiti*, *yatit*, *yetit*, *yitit*, just here, here in this very place; so *yot*, *yotut*, *yor*, *yuri; yām*, as soon as; *tām*, then; *yāmatai*, *tāmatai*, just then. *-i*, *-ai*, *-oi*, *-ui*, are also added to *yuth*, *yut*, *yats*, etc.; *yuthui* or *yuthoi*, in this very manner; so *yutui* or *yutoi*, *yitsai*, etc.

Yyuth, *hyuth*, *kyuth*, *tyuth; yut*, *hut*, *kut*, *tyut;* and *yats*, *hats*, *kats*, *tats*, are regularly declined. The plural of *yut*, etc., will mean "many;" as, *yiti lafz*, so many words. *Yats* is often used for "more;" as, *yats tser*, more late, latter.

127.

	Near Demonstrative.	More Remote Demonstrative.	Interrogative.	Relative.	Correlative.	Meaning.
	yih (yėmis, yath)	huh (hoh, humis)	kus (kas, kath)?	yus (yė-mis, yas, yath)	suh (tas, tath)	*this*, *that*, *who?* *who*, *he*
Time	wun, woni	ati	kar?	yeli	teli	*now*, *then*, *when*, etc.
	wuniuktām	hutām	kartām?	yutām	tutām	*till now*, *till then*, *till when*, etc.
Place	yiti, yeti	huti	kati?	yati, yeti	tati, teti	*here*, *in this very place*, *there*, etc.
	yȯt, yut	hȯt, hut	kȯt? kut?	yȯt, yut	tȯt, tut	*here*, *there*, *where*, etc.
	yor, yorạ	hor, horạ	kor? korạ?	yor, yorạ	tor, torạ	*hither*, *hence*; *thither*, *thence*; *whither*, *whence*, etc.
Manner	yuth	hyuth (hiu)	kyuth?	yuth	tyuth	*such*, *so*, *as*, *like*
Quantity	yut	hut	kut?	yut	tyut	*this much*, *that much*, *how much*, etc.; plu. *many*
Number	yats	hats	kats?	yats	tats	*so many*, *that many*, *how many*, etc.

128. (1) *Relating to Time.*

Ada, then.
Ākhir, *patau lākan*, at last.
Arvạ patạ, at length.
Az, *aji*, to-day.
Dohai, *prat doha*, *hamesha*, always.
Kolkiet, day after to-morrow.
Otar, or *utar*, day before yesterday.
Paga, to-morrow.
Parus, last year.
Răt, last night.
Rets, *subhas*, *subhanas*, early, in the morning.
Yawa, yesterday.
Yihus, this year.
Za, ever.
Za na, never.
Za nata za, some time or other.

129. (2) *Relating to Place.*

Andar, *andara*, within, inside.
Apor, *aporkun*, that side.
Dachan kun, right-hand side.
Har kuni, everywhere.
Khowur kun, left-hand side.
Kuni, anywhere.
Kuni na, nowhere.
Nebar, *nebara*, outside.
Yipor, *yipor kun*, this side.

130. (3) *Relating to Manner.*

Ak ak, singly, one by one.
Aki lati, or *aki pheri*, once, one time.
Algöbi, by chance.

Dewa, perhaps.
Kèta pöṭh, how.
Padi pètha padi, or *padi path padi*, step by step, by degrees.
Sètha, much, very.
Sot sot, slowly.
Ṭakān ṭakān, quickly.
Tsor, much.
Wāra, skilfully, well.
Wāra wāra, slowly.
Yaqīnan, in truth, certainly.
Yats, more.
Yot, only.
Yiti pöṭh, in this way.

131. The common adverbs of affirmation and negation in use are *awạ*, yes, and *nạ*, no; but others are also used which are more respectful—

Ahansạ, yes, sir (spoken to an equal or superior).

Ahanbin, yes, madam (spoken to an equal or superior).

Nạdid, respectful, used in speaking to a mother or elderly female.

Nau (masc.), *nāi* (fem.), no certainly.

With the imperative *ma* is used instead of *nạ*; as, *ma kar*, do not; *ma wan*, do not speak.

132. (For the adverbial participle, see the verb.)

2. Prepositions.

133. Prepositions in Kashmīrī are used after nouns, which they govern in the dative (locative) or genitive case. Those that govern the genitive case are mostly nouns used as prepositions.

The following are the principal prepositions in general use:—

134. (1) *Those governing Nouns in the Dative or Locative Case.*

Andar, in.
Andiạnd, around, alongside.
Andkin, close by.
Athi, by hand.
Barăbar, equal to.
Bontakani, in front of.
Bronṭ, or *bonth*, before.
Dachankun, on the right-hand side.
Hiuh, *hyuh*, or *hish*, like.
Kėt, upon, in.
Khowarkun, on the left-hand side.
Kin, by the side of.
Kiut, *kits*, for.
Kun, towards, in the direction of.
Manz, in.
Manzbăg, in the middle.
Nakhạ, near.
Nakhatal, close by.
Nazdīk, near.
Nėbar, outside.
Nish, near.
Păsa, for the sake of.
Path, *pathkani*, behind.
Pėṭh, upon.
Săn, with.
Sivöi, without, except.
Tal, below, under.
Waröi, except.

135. (2) *Those governing Nouns in the Genitive Case.*

Badaḷạ, in place of.
Băpat, about, concerning.

Khoṭa, than, compared with.
Khötira, for, on account of (*vide* par. 138).
Nāwa, for the sake of, for the name of.
Taraf, towards; *tarafa*, from towards.
Wasīla, by means of.
Wasīlasöt, by means of.

136. (3) *Those governing Nouns in the Ablative Case.*

Andara, from, from under or in.
Bāpat, concerning, about.
Khötira, for the sake of.
Manza, from, from inside.
Manzbāga, from, from the middle.
Nebara, from, from outside.
Nishi, from, from near.
Pètha, from, from upon.
Rust, without, not having.
Sān, with.
Söti, with, by means of.
Tarafa, from, from the side of.

137. Generally those prepositions govern the ablative case which denote motion from; and most of the prepositions which govern the locative case, denoting place, by having an *a* or *i* added to them, will then denote motion from that place. Thus, *garas andar* means "in the house;" but *gara andara* is "from in the house."

138. When the prepositions *nishi* and *sān* are used with singular nouns of the second declension, which are names of persons or animals, except proper nouns, then they take the *s*; as, *Suh chhu sahibas nishi āmut*, He has come from the sahib; but when the nouns represent inanimate objects, then they simply take *a* before these prepositions; as, *Suh chhu bāgha nishi āmut*, He has come from the garden.

Nouns used with the preposition *khötirą*, if they represent animate objects, take the regular genitive, *sund*, *hund*, etc.; as, *sahib[i]sąnd[i] khötirą*, for the sake of the sahib; but when they represent inanimate objects they take only the *ą*; as, *kalamą khötira*, for the sake of a pen.

(For further remarks on the prepositions, see Syntax.)

139. Besides the above prepositions, the following Arabic and Persian prefixes are sometimes used, especially by Muhammadāns, with words from those languages:—

Az, from, by.
'An, from.
'Alā, upon, above.
Bā, with.
Ba, in, by.
Bar, on, in, at.
Barāe, for, on account of.
Be, without.
Bilā, without.
Dar, in, within.
Fi, in.
Illā, except, besides.
Ka, according to.
La, *li*, to, for.
Ma', with.
Min, from.
Muṭābiq, conformable to.
Mujib or *bamujib*, by means of.

3. Conjunctions.

140. There is nothing to be noted particularly about the conjunctions. Of those following, the ones in the first list are peculiar to Kashmīrī, and those in the second list are common to both Kashmīrī and Hindustānī, and are chiefly used by the Muhammadāns:—

(1) *Conjunctions used only in Kashmīrī.*

Ai, or *harga*, if.
Ada, then.
Beyi, again.
Kyāzi, or *tikyāzi*, for, because.
Nata, otherwise.
Tą, and.
Ti, also.
Yadante, although.
Yātai, either, or.

Yod, *yadante*, *yadwai*, *yadwanai*, although, notwithstanding.

Yuth, in order that.

Zan, as if.

Zi, that.

141. (2) *Conjunctions common to Kashmīrī and Hindustānī.*

Agar, *gar*, if.

Agarchi, although.

Amma, but, moreover.

Balki, but, on the contrary.

Goya, as if.

Hālānki, whereas, notwithstanding.

Hanoz, yet, still,

Harchand, although.

Lekin, but.

Magar, but, except.

Pas, therefore, thence.

Par, but, yet.

Yā, or, either.

4. Interjections.

142. The words placed before nouns in the vocative case are—

Word	Gender	Use
Hā!	masc.	Used generally to inferiors.
Hai!	masc.	
Hatā!	masc.	
Hato!	masc.	
Heyo!	masc.	
Ho!	masc.	
Hatöi!	fem.	
Hatāi!	fem.	
Heyöi!	fem.	
Hataba!	masc.	Used in addressing equals.
Habin!	fem.	
Hatabin!	fem.	
Hatasạ!	masc. and fem.	
Haz!	masc.	Used in addressing superiors.
Hadèd!	fem.	
Shāh!	masc.	

Haz! for *hazrat!* O saint! and is used only by Muhammadāns. *Dėd*, mother; *bin* for *beni*, sister; *sa* for *sāhib* or *sāhiba*; *shāh* for *pādshāh*; and *bā* for *boi*, brother.

143. The following are some of the words often heard as exclamations used by the Kashmīrīs:—

Afsos! alas!
Ai! O! *Ai Khudāya!* or *Ai Khudāyo!* O God!
Ābrāi! bless you!
Balāi lage! thy misfortune be upon me!
Hāi! alas!
Hosh kar! / *Khabardār!* } take care!
Kya zabar! how good! wonderful!
Kya gom! what has happened to me!
Shābāsh! or *shāhbāsh!* well done!
Tauba! shame! repent! fie!
Wā wā! O fie!
Wāi! alas!

CHAPTER VII.

NUMBERS.

1. Cardinals.

144. Although numerals are adjectives, yet, as there are many points in them that need explanation, it is, perhaps, more convenient to treat of them in a separate chapter.

145. The cardinal numbers are—

1 = *ak*.
2 = *zạ*, or *zạh*.
3 = *trė*, or *trėh*.
4 = *tsor*.
5 = *pānts*, or *pönts*.
6 = *shė*, or *shėh*.
7 = *sat*.
8 = *öth*.
9 = *nau*.
10 = *da*, *dah*.
11 = *ka*, *kah*.
12 = *ba*, *bah*.
13 = *trua*, *truah*.
14 = *tsȏda*, *tsȏdah*.
15 = *panda*, *pandah*.
16 = *shura*, *shurah*.

17 = *sada*, *sadah*.
18 = *arda*, *ardah*.
19 = *kunawuh*.
20 = *wuh*.
21 = *akạwuh*.
22 = *zạtowuh*.
23 = *trowuh*.
24 = *tsòwuh*.
25 = *pũṇtsạ*.
26 = *shèwuh*.
27 = *satāwuh*.
28 = *öṭhöwuh*.
29 = *kunạtrạ*.
30 = *trạ*.
31 = *akạtrạ*.
32 = *dotrạ*.
33 = *titrạ*.
34 = *tsòyitra*.
35 = *pāntsạtrạ*.
36 = *sheyitrạ*.
37 = *satạtrạ*.
38 = *arạtrạ*.
39 = *kunạtöji*.
40 = *tsataji*.
41 = *akạtöji*, or *akạtöj*.
42 = *dòitöji*, *dòitöj*.
43 = *titöji*, *titöj*.
44 = *tsòitöji*, *tsòitöj*.
45 = *pāntsạtöji*.
46 = *shèitöji*.
47 = *satạtöji*.
48 = *arạtöji*.
49 = *kunạwanza*.
50 = *pantsa*.
51 = *akạwanza*, or *akwanz*.
52 = *duwanza*, or *duwanz*.
53 = *trèwanza*, or *trèwanz*.
54 = *tsuwanza*, or *tsuwanz*.
55 = *pāntsạwanza*, or *pānts-wanz*.
56 = *shiwanza*, or *shiwanz*.
57 = *satạwanza*, or *satwanz*.
58 = *arạwanza*, or *awanz*.
59 = *kunahöṭh*.
60 = *sheṭh*.
61 = *akạhöṭh*.
62 = *duhöṭh*.
63 = *trèhöṭh*.
64 = *tsuhöṭh*.
65 = *pāntsạhöṭh*.
66 = *shihöṭh*.
67 = *satạhöṭh*.
68 = *arạhöṭh*.
69 = *kunạsatat*.
70 = *satat*.
71 = *akạsatat*.
72 = *dusatat*.
73 = *trèsatat*.
74 = *tsusatat*.
75 = *pantsạsatat*.
76 = *shisatat*.
77 = *satạsatat*.
78 = *arạsatat*.
79 = *kunạshīth*.
80 = *shīth*.
81 = *akạshīth*.
82 = *dushīth*, *dòishīth*.
83 = *trishīth*.

84 = *tsushīth.*
85 = *pāntsashīth.*
86 = *shishīth.*
87 = *satashīth.*
88 = *arashīth.*
89 = *kunanamat.*
90 = *namat.*
91 = *akanamat*, or *aknum.*
92 = *dunamat*, or *dunam.*
93 = *tranamat, trènamat*, or *trènam.*
94 = *tsunamat*, or *tsunam.*
95 = *pantsanamat*, or *pantsnam.*
96 = *shinamat*, or *shinam.*
97 = *satanamat*, or *satnam.*
98 = *aranamat*, or *arnam.*
99 = *namanamat*, or *namanam*, or *namānum.*
100 = *hat*, or *hath.*
101 = *ak hath ta ak.*
102 = *ak hath ta za.*
1000 = *sās.*
100,000 = *lach.*
10,000,000 = *kror*, or *karor.*
100,000,000 = *abad.*
100,000,000,000 = *kharab*, or innumerable.

146. In counting, Kashmīrīs always call one *barakat;* this is to bring good luck.

147. *Ak* is declined like a masculine noun of the second declension, but the fem. *ach* like a feminine noun of the third declension. All other numbers follow the plural of the first declension. *Akoi*, or *akui*, etc., is intensive, meaning "only one."

148. There are two words used to express indefiniteness—*mara* and *khand*, meaning "about;" the former used with numbers, and the latter with weights and measures; as, *pandah mara mahiniu*, about fifteen men; *namat mara guri*, about ninety horses; *khār khand*, about a khār (khār, or kharwār, is an ass-load); *trak khand*, about a trak (about sixteen traks make a kharwār, and a trak contains about five seers).

149. Indefiniteness can also be expressed by using two numbers together without any conjunction; thus, *tsor pānts*, four or five; *hat za hat*, one or two hundred.

150. **2. Ordinals.**

First,	*godanyuk* (masc.),	*godanyich* (fem.).	
Second,	*doyum* ,,	*doyim*	,,
Third,	*treyum* ,,	*treyim*	,,
Fourth,	*tsoryum* ,,	*tsoryim*	,,
Fifth,	*pāntsyum* ,,	*pāntsyim*	,,
Sixth,	*sheyum* ,,	*sheyim*	,,
Seventh,	*satyum* ,,	*satim*, or *satyim*	(fem.).
Eighth,	*öthyum* ,,	*öthim*, or *öthyim*	,,
Ninth,	*nauyum* ,,	*navim*, or *nauyim*	,,
Tenth,	*dahyum* ,,	*dahim*, or *dahyim*	,,

In this way all other ordinals are regularly formed from the cardinals.

3. Aggregate or Collective Numbers.

151. In speaking of separate numbers, slightly modified forms are used; as—

Za aki, two ones.
Za trāna, two threes.
Trèh tsăk, three fours.
Ak pònz, one five.
Trèh panzi, three fives.
Ak shak, one six.
Trèh shaka, three sixes.
Trèh öthi, three eights.
Ak nau or *nam*, one nine.
Za dahi, two tens.
Kuri, a score, twenty.

152. The word *-bod* (masc. sing.), *-bad* (fem. sing.), *-badi* (masc. plu.), *-bòza* (fem. plu.), is added to *hat*, *sās*, *lach*, *karor*, etc.; as, *hatabadi*, hundreds; *sāsabadi*, thousands; *lachabadi*, lakhs; *karorabadi*, krors.

153. Distributives are formed by repeating the number without any conjunction between them; as, *ak ak*, one by one; *za za*, two by two, by twos; *tsor tsor*, by fours, etc.

154. Proportional numbers are formed by adding *-gun* to

the cardinals, the first four undergoing a slight change; thus—

Ogun	(masc.),	*ogan*	(fem.),	onefold.
Dogun	"	*dogan*	"	twofold.
Trègun	"	*trègan*	"	threefold.
Tsogun	"	*tsogan*	"	fourfold.
Pantsgun	"	*pantsgan*	"	fivefold.
Shègun	"	*shègan*	"	sixfold, etc.

155. Time, or turn, is expressed by annexing *-lati* or *-phiri* to the cardinals when the number of times is to be indicated, and to the ordinals when any particular turn or time is meant; as, *aki lati*, or *aki phiri*, one time, or turn; *tsori lati*, or *tsori phiri*, four times, or turns; *doyimi lati*, or *doyimi phiri*, the second time, or turn, etc.

156. 4. Fractional Numbers.

$\frac{1}{2}$ = *od* (masc. sing.), *ad* (fem. sing.), *adi* (masc. plu.), *aji* (fem. plu.), one-half.

$\frac{1}{4}$ = *tsorim hissa* or *pau*, one quarter.

$\frac{3}{4}$ = *dun* (masc. sing.), *dan* (fem. sing.), one quarter less (than one)—three quarters.

$1\frac{1}{4}$ = *swād*, one and a quarter.

$1\frac{1}{2}$ = *dòd* (masc. sing.), *dad* (fem. sing.), etc., one and a half.

$1\frac{3}{4}$ = *dun za*, a quarter less than two—one and three quarters.

$2\frac{1}{4}$ = *swād za*, two and a quarter.

$2\frac{1}{2}$ = *dāi*, or *sāda za*, two and a half.

$3\frac{1}{2}$ = *sāda trè*, three and a half.

75 = *dun hat*, a quarter less than a hundred—seventy-five.

125 = *swād hat*, one and a quarter hundreds—a hundred and twenty-five.

150 = *dòd hat*, one and a half hundred—a hundred and fifty.

175 = *dun zạ hat*, a quarter less than two hundreds—a hundred and seventy-five.

250 = *dāi hat*, two and a half hundreds—two hundred and fifty.

5. Divisions of Time.

157. (1) *Days of the Week.*

English.	Kashmīrī.	Sanskrit.	Hindī.
Sunday	Ātwār	Kavivāra	Itwār
Monday	Tsandawār	Somavāra	Somwār
Tuesday	Bomwār	Mangalavāra	Mangal
Wednesday	Bodhwār	Budhavāra	Budh
Thursday	Braswār	Vṛihaspativāra	Biphai
Friday	Jum'a, *or* Shukarwār	Śukravāra	Suk
Saturday	Batawār	Śanivāra	Sanīchar

158. A whole day and night of twenty-four hours is divided into eight parts, or watches; the day into four parts beginning about sunrise, and the night into four parts beginning at sunset; they call these the first or second, etc., watch (*pahar*) of the day, and the first or second, etc., watch (*pahar*) of the night.

159. (2) *Months of the Year.*

English.	Kashmīrī.	Hindī.
April–May	Vạhek	Vaiśākh
May–June	Zèṭh	Jeṭh
June–July	Hāṛh	Āshāṛh
July–August	Shrāwun	Śrāvan
August–September	Bhādirpèṭh	Bhādra

ENGLISH.	KASHMĪRĪ.	HINDĪ.
September–October	Āshid	Āśivin, *or* Āsin
October–November	Kārttik	Karttik
November–December	Mȯnjhor	Āgrahāyaṇ, *or* Agahan
December–January	Pȯh	Paush, *or* Pūs
January–February	Māgh	Māgh
February–March	Phāgun, *or* Fāgun	Phāgun
March–April	Tsitaṛ	Chaitra, *or* Chait

160. The Hindu year is solar, and is divided into twelve parts, or months, beginning with Vaḥek, or Vaiśākh, about the 11th or 12th of April; but the Muhammadān year is lunar, and is divided into twelve lunar months, beginning with Muharram. As most of the inhabitants of Kashmīr are Muhammadāns, and they must know the Muhammadān days of the week and months of the year in order to keep their feasts and fasts, the Arabic names of the months, and the Hindustānī and Persian names of the days of the week, which are often used in Kashmīr, are subjoined—

(3) *Days of the Week.*

ENGLISH.	HINDUSTĀNĪ.	PERSIAN.
Sunday	Itwār	Yakshamba
Monday	Somwār, *or* Pīr	Doshamba
Tuesday	Mangal	Sishamba
Wednesday	Budh	Chārshamba
Thursday	Jum'a rāt	Panjshamba
Friday	Jum'a	Ādīna, *or* Jum'a
Saturday	Sanīchar	Shan, *or* Hafta

(4) *Arabic Lunar Months.*

1. Muharram, 30 days.
2. Ṣafar, 29 days.
3. Rabī-ul-awwal, 30 days.
4. Rabī' uṣ-ṣāni, *or* Rabī'-ul-ākhir, 30 days.
5. Jumād-al-awwal, 30 days.
6. Jumād-aṣ-ṣāni, *or* Jumād-al-ākhir, 29 days.
7. Rajab, 30 days.
8. Sha'bān, 29 days.
9. Ramazān, 30 days.
10. Shawwāl, 29 days.
11. Ẓī, l Qa'da, *or* Zī Qa'da, 30 days.
12. Zī, l Ḥijja, *or* Zī Ḥijja, 29 days.

(5) *Ages and Eras.*

161. The Hindus generally believe in four great periods, or ages, the three first of which are past, so that we are now living in the fourth, or last.

1. Satyayug,	comprising	1,728,000	years.
2. Treta,	„	1,296,000	„
3. Dwāpar,	„	864,000	„
4. Kaliyug,	„	432,000	„

162. The Kaliyug is said to have commenced B.C. 3102. At its close, some 427,000 years hence, after a general deterioration, there is to be a universal destruction.

163. The era Samvat is also in common use amongst Hindus, and dates from B.C. 57.

164. The era in universal use amongst Musalmāns is the Hijra, the date of Muhammad's flight from Mecca to Medīna, A.D. 622. As the Muhammadān year consists of twelve

lunations amounting to little more than 354 days, their New Year's Day will consequently happen every year about eleven days earlier than in the preceding year.*

CHAPTER VIII.

DERIVATION OF WORDS.

165. It has been stated that, taking a hundred ordinary Kashmīrī words, they will be found to be derived from the following languages, in about the following proportions :—

Derived from		Sanskrit	25
„	„	Persian	40
„	„	Hindustānī	15
„	„	Arabic	10
„	„	Tibetān, Turkī, and others	10
			100

These figures were most probably supplied by Muhammadāns, who would, of course, use more Persian and less Sanskrit words than the Hindus.

166. Some pundits in Kashmīr, after considerable reflection and consultation with their friends, gave me the following proportions :—

Words	derived	from	Sanskrit and Prakrit ..	35
„	„	„	Urdu, Hindī, and Punjābī	20
„	„	„	Persian	25
„	„	„	Arabic	10
„	„	„	Ladākī, Turkī, and others	10
				100

* There are two simple rules for finding what year A.D. (Christian) corresponds with any year A.H. (Muhammadān).

Rule 1. $\text{A.H.} - \frac{\text{A.H.} \times 3}{100} + 621{\cdot}54 = \text{A.D.}$

Rule 2. $(\text{A.H.} \times {\cdot}97) + 621{\cdot}54 = \text{A.D.}$ This is more accurate than the other.

1. Prefixes.

167. Some of the most common prefixes in use in Kashmīrī are—

A-, *an-*, not; as, *pôz*, true, *apôz*, not true, untrue; *pôzior*, truthful, *apôzior*, untruthful; *dur*, strong, *adur*, not strong, weak; *hohurmut*, a married man, *anhohur*, a bachelor; *herishmats*, a married woman, *anharish*, a virgin.

Bad-, bad, evil; as, *duạ*, a prayer, *badduạ*, a curse; *nām*, a name, *badnām*, a bad name, infamous; *hāl*, condition, *badhāl*, bad condition.

Be-, without, not; as, *tämīz*, conscience, discrimination, *betamīz*, without conscience or discrimination; *hosh*, sense, feeling, *behosh*, without sense, senseless; so *beṣabar*, impatient; *beaql* (*beqal*), without understanding.

Ghair- (*gair-*), not, different, without, foreign; as, *hāzir*, present, *ghairḥāzir*, not present, absent; *mumkin*, possible, *ghairmumkin*, impossible; *wājib*, right, just, *ghairwājib*, unjust, wrong.

Kam-, deficient, little; as, *bakht*, fortune, luck, *kambakht*, unfortunate; *fahm*, understanding, *kamfahm*, of little understanding.

Kô-, depreciation, disparagement; as, *karm*, an action, *kôkarm*, a bad action; *zāt*, nature, disposition, *kôzāt*, of bad nature or disposition; *dôh*, a day, *kôdôh*, an unlucky day; *nechu*, a child, *kônechu*, a bad child.

Lā-, not; as, *chāra*, help, *lāchār*, helpless, *lāchārī*, helplessness.

Nā-, not; as, *khush* (*khôsh*) happy, *nākhush*, unhappy.

Ne-, *ner-*, *nīr-*, without, not; as, *nebagor*, cooked without oil or ghee; *mal*, dirt, *nermal*, clean, clear; *āsh*, hope, *nerāsh*, hopeless; *dān*, riches, *nerdān*, poor; *dush*, a fault, *nirdush*, faultless.

Parā-, back, implies defect; as, *ādhīn*, humble, *parādhīn*, dependence.

Par-, or *wòpar-*, other, different, foreign, strange; as, *des*, a country, *pardes*, a foreign country; *lok*, a world, *parilok*, the next world; *dīn*, religion, *pardīn*, a foreign religion; *mahiniu*, a man, *parmahiniu*, a stranger, *wòparmahiniu*, also a stranger.

2. Affixes.

(1) *Derivative Nouns.*

168. (*a*) *Nouns of Agency and Possession.*

-āl; as, *har*, a fight, *haral*, a fighter; *lat*, a kick, *latal*, a kicker; *yaḍ*, belly, *yiḍal*, a glutton.

-bān, *-bānạ*, *-wān*; as, *bāg* (*bāgh*), a garden, *bāgbān*, a gardener, or *bāgwān*; *khwar*, a foot, *khwarạbānạ*, a shoe; *batạ*, food, *khènạ*, eating, *batạbānạ*, or *khènạbānạ*, a plate.

-band; as, *n'al*, a horse-shoe, *n'alband*, a farrier, or shoeing-smith.

-bāz; as, *kotar*, a pigeon, *kotarbāz*, one who trains pigeons.

-chi; as, *mash'al*, a torch, *mash'ālchī*, a torch-bearer.

-dānạ; as, *kalam*, a pen, *kalamdānạ*, that which contains pens; *tāp*, sunshine, *tapạdānạ*, that which keeps off the sunshine, an umbrella.

-dār; as, *zamīn*, land, *zamīndār*, one who tills or owns land.

-gār; as, *gunāh*, sin, *gunāhgār*, a sinner.

-kār; as, *bad*, bad, *badkār*, an evil-doer.

-lad; as, *miònd*, leprosy, *meṇdilad*, a leper; *hètar*, a skin-disease, *hètarilad*, one afflicted with hètar; *wòpas*, hunger, starvation, *wòpaslad*, one who is starving.

-sāz; as, *jāl*, a net, snare, *jālsāz*, a deceiver.

-ūr, or *-gūr*; as, *sòn*, gold, *sònūr*, a goldsmith; *ts̱òm*, leather, *ts̱òmūr*, a shoemaker; *jild*, a cover or binding of a book, *jildạgur*, a bookbinder.

-wār; as, *ummed*, hope, *ummedwār*, one who hopes, a candidate.

-wol, or *-wun*, added to any verb; as, *parun*, to read, *paranwol* or *parawun*, a reader, one about to read.

169. (*b*) *Nouns denoting Place.*

-ābād; as, *Islāmābād*, the place or town of Islām; *Shāhābād*, or *Shāhbād*, the place of a king.

-bal; as, *Hazratbal*, the place of Hazrat, or his Highness; *Yārabal*, the place of a friend, a landing-place, or ghāt.

-nagar; as, *Srinagar*, the place or city of Sri (the sun); *Rāmnagar*, the city of Rām (Rāma).

-pur; as, *Nawapur*, the place of boats; *Rambīr Singhpur*, the place or town of Rambir Singh.

*-wan*ⁱ; as, *Kuliwan*ⁱ, the place of trees.

-zār; as, *Poshizār*, the place of flowers; *Kandizār*, the place of thorns.

170. (*c*) *Abstract Nouns.*

-ar; as, *tiōt*, bitter, *techar*, bitterness; *thōd*, high, *thazar*, height; *tsōt*, short, *tsōchar*, shortness.

-chār; as, *lōkut*, little, *lōkutchār*, littleness.

-chī; as, *bōch*, hungry, *bōchī*, hunger.

-er; as, *mōdur*, sweet, *mōdrer*, sweetness; *hōndur*, cold, *hōndrer*, coldness.

-gī; as, *shur*, a child, *shurigī*, childishness; *tāza*, fresh, *tāzagī*, freshness.

-ī; as, *garm*, hot, *garmī*, heat; *kam*, little, *kamī*, deficiency.

-il; as *shur*, a child, *shuril*, childishness.

171. (*d*) *Diminutive Nouns.*

-hun, *-han*, are often added to nouns to express diminution or endearment; as, *nechu*, a boy, *nechiuhun*, a little boy;

kur, a girl, *korihan*, a little girl; *lur*, a staff, *lorihan*, a stick, or small staff; *tsȯṭ*, bread, a loaf, *tsȯchihan*, a little loaf.

172. (2) *Derivative Adjectives.*

-*āwar*; as, *zor*, strength, *zorāwar*, strong.
-*dār*; as, *wafa*, fidelity, *wafadār*, faithful.
-*gīn*; as, *gam* (*gham*), sorrow, *gamgīn*, sorrowful.
-*gīr*; as, *dil*, heart, *dilgīr*, grieved.
-*hȯt*; as, *tresh*, thirst, *treshihȯt*, thirsty; *bȯchi*, hunger, *bȯchihȯt*, hungry.
-*mand*; as, *doulat*, wealth, *doulatmand*, wealthy.
-*nāk*; as, *haul*, terror, *haulnāk*, terrible.
-*warȯi*; as, *gāsh*, light, *gāshiwarȯi*, without light, blind; *ath*, a hand, *athạwarȯi*, without hands.

(3) *Derivative Verbs.*

173. (*a*) *From Adjectives.*

Bȯḍ, great; *bȯḍun*, to be great.
Hȯkh, dry; *hȯkhun*, to be dry; *hȯkhanāwun*, to make dry.
Nau, new; *nāwun*, to be new.
Niuk, thin; *nyikun*, to be thin.
Siud, straight; *sidun*, to be straight.
Thȯd, large, tall; *thadun*, to be tall.
Tiȯt, bitter; *tètun*, to be bitter.
Tsȯk, sour; *tsȯkun*, to be sour.
Ziut, long; *zetun*, to be long.

174. (*b*) *From Nouns.*

Dag, a blow; *dagun*, to strike.
Dor, a course, racecourse; *dorun*, to run.
Gand, a knot; *gandun*, to tie, bind.
Hār, defeat; *hārun*, to lose.

Lār, flight; *lārun*, to flee, to run after.
Mār, murder; *mārun*, to kill.
Mandach, shame; *mandachun*, to be ashamed.
Sher, arrangement, head; *sherun*, to accomplish, set in order.
Tār, side, bank; *tārun*, to take to the side, ferry.
Tol, a weight; *tolun*, to weigh.
Wāt, a seam: *wātun*, to join.
Yār, a friend; *yārun*, to be friendly.

3. Compound Words.

These are principally formed by joining together two nouns or a noun and an adjective.

175. (1) *Two Nouns.*

Athạpanji, a glove; from *ath*, a hand, and *panji*, the fingers.
Dôdạshur, an infant; from *dôd*, milk, and *shur*, a child.
Dun-dach, walnut grape, a particular kind of grape; from *dun*, a walnut, and *dach*, a grape.
Gāda-shikār, fishing; from *gāḍ*, a fish, and *shikār*, hunting.
Gantbror, a kite (paper); from *gant*, a kite (bird), and *bror*, a cat.
Gogajihāk, turnip-tops; from *gogaj*, a turnip, and *hāk*, green vegetables.
Huniwushuk, tares; from *hun*, a dog, and *wushuk*, barley.
Indarmöhal, the long beam by which the Kashmīrīs pound rice by standing on it at one end, and working it up and down; from *indar*, a wheel, and *möhal*, a pestle.
Kanas-dod, ear-ache; from *kan*, the ear, and *dod*, pain.
Kanạwöj, an ear-ring; from *kan*, the ear, and *wöj*, a ring.
Kandạrwāṇ, a baker's shop; from *kandur*, a baker, and *wāṇ*, a shop; so *puzwāṇ*, a butcher's shop, and *rangạrwāṇ*, a dyer's shop; from *puz*, a butcher, and *rangur*, a dyer.
Kaṭạmāz, mutton; from *kaṭ*, a sheep, and *māz*, flesh.

Kāwa-dach, a black kind of grape; from *kāwa*, a crow, and *dach*, a grape.

Laṭitāruk, a comet; from *laṭ*, a tail, and *tāruk*, a star.

Mėṯsihāṇz, a boatman who sells earth; from *mėṯs*, earth, and *hāṇz*, a boatman; so *dungahāṇz*, a boatman of a dunga; *bahaṯsạhāṇz*, a boatman of a bahaṯs; *dembạhāṇz*, a boatman who sells the vegetables that grow on the small islands called Demb; *zinihāṇz*, a boatman who sells ziun (fire-wood).

Mol-mōj, parents; literally, "father, mother."

Nathwōj, a nose-ring; from *nath*, nose, and *wōz*, a ring.

Rātạkrōl, a bat; from *rāt*, night, and *krōl*, an insect.

Rātạmogẖal, an owl; from *rāt*, and *mogẖal*.

Rudạwonⁱ, rain-water; from *rud*, rain, and *wonⁱ*, water; so *krariwonⁱ*, well-water; *vėthạwonⁱ*, river-water.

Ṯsunṭ-kul, an apple tree; from *ṯsunṭ*, an apple, and *kul*, a tree; so *bamṯsunṭ-kul*, a quince tree, etc.

Wushukwāt, coarsely ground barley; from *wushuk*, barley, and *wāt*, a seam; so *makaiwāt*, *kanakwāt*, coarsely ground Indian corn and wheat.

Wuṯsagagur, a flying fox; from *wuḍun*, to fly, and *gagur*, a rat; so *usgagur*, a flying squirrel.

176. (2) *An Adjective and Noun.*

Anạgagur, a musk-rat; from *ȯn*, blind, and *gagur*, a rat.

Chaṯsạkol, the name of a small river near Srinagar; from *chiȯt*, white, and *kȯl*, a stream.

Kạṭạkol, a winter stream, dry in the hot weather; from *kạṭạ*, false, unreal, and *kȯl*, a stream.

Tėṭạvenạ, a particular kind of grass; from *tiȯt*, bitter, and *vien*, grass.

Tsȯkạladur, the name of an edible root; from *ṯsȯk*, sour, and *ladur*, a root.

Tsȯk-bamtsunṭ, sour-quince, the name of a particular kind of quince; so *mȯdur-bamtsunṭ*, sweet-quince; *teṭha-tsera*, a particular kind of apricot (bitter); *tsokạ-tsera*, ditto (sour); *modur-tsunṭ*, a particular kind of apple (sweet); *tsoka-tsunṭ*, ditto (sour); *modur-tsunun*, a particular kind of peach (sweet); *tiȯt-tsunun*, ditto (bitter); *tsȯkạ-ṭānj*, a particular kind of pear (sour); *modar-ṭānj*, ditto (sweet).

177. Muhammadāns often use pure Persian or Arabic compounds; as, *āmad-o-raft*, intercourse; *dīda-o-dānista*, intentionally, deliberately; *jahān-panāh*, your Majesty; *guft-o-shanud*, or *guft-o-gu*, conversation; *āb-i-haiyāt*, water of life; *āb-o-hawā*, climate, etc.

CHAPTER IX.

SYNTAX.

178. SYNTAX ("arranging together") treats of the arrangement of words in a sentence. Every sentence necessarily consists of two parts—a *subject*, that of which something is affirmed or denied; and a *predicate*, that which is affirmed or denied of the subject.

179. The subject must be a noun, with or without qualifying words, or the equivalent of a noun; an infinitive verb; a phrase; or a sentence. The predicate must be a verb, with or without qualifying words or phrases.

1. ORDER OF WORDS IN A SENTENCE.

180. The general rule observed in the arrangement of words in a simple sentence in Kashmīrī is the same as in English: *Nār chhu garm*, Fire is hot; *Kul chhu thȯd*, The tree is high; *Mahniu chhu rut*, The man is good; *Mahniv sund lokut*

nechu chhu parān, The man's little son is reading; *Pādshāh-sanz bòhödur* (*bahādur*) *lashkar chhè ḥāzir*, The king's brave army is present; *Mahniu chhu lāyān guris*, or *Mahniu chhu guris lāyān*, The man is beating the horse; *Bòḍ mahniu chhu lāyān lokatis nechivis*, or *Bòḍ mahiniu chhu lokatis nechivis lāyān*, The (or, a) big man beats (or, is beating) the little son.

181. From the above examples it will be seen that a noun in the genitive case usually precedes its governing noun, and an adjective the substantive that it qualifies.

2. Substitutes for the Article.

182. There are no words in the Kashmīrī language exactly answering to the articles "a," "an," and "the;" the word *posh*, flower, may mean "a flower" or "the flower."

183. To imply indefiniteness we may use (1) the simple noun; (2) the noun with the affix *-ā*; (3) or we may use *ak* or *akā*, one, or *kāṇh* or *kèṇh*, some, before the noun; as, *nechu*, boy, or, a boy; *mahnivā*, a man, any man; *kāṇh mahniu*, some man; *Mezas pèth chhè kitābā*, There is some book on the table.

184. When definiteness is required, the English definite article may be represented by the demonstrative pronouns; as, *yih mahniu*, this man; *huh mahniu*, that man; *hòh zanānạ*, that woman; *suh gur*, that horse; *sòh kitāb*, that book; *Suh mahniu chhu nākārạ tạ kharāb*, That man is worthless and bad.

3. Nouns.

Concord of one Substantive with another.

185. When one substantive is placed in juxtaposition with another, or with a personal pronoun, for the purpose of explaining or describing it, then it is put by apposition in the same number, gender, and case; as, *Māhārāj sāhib*, *Kāshīrī*

hund hākim, chhu bīmār, The Māhārāja, the ruler of Kashmīr, is ill.

186. Titles, and most terms signifying the higher professions, when used with proper names, are placed before them; as, *Māhārāj Golāb Singh, Rājā Moti Singh, Qāzi Nasīr-ud-Dīn, Maulavī Nizām-ud-Dīn, Munshi Nur-ud-Dīn, Dīwān Anant Rām, Pundit Rāmjiu.*

187. The word *pundit,* when required, must always be used before any proper name having *-jiu, -bat, -kol, -tiuk, -rām, -dar, -munish,* etc., which describe the caste or family; but if the proper name have no such word affixed to it, then the word *pundit* may be used after it; as, *Prakāsh pundit.*

188. The names of trades and all inferior occupations follow the name of the person; as, *Raḥmān chān,* Raḥmān the carpenter; *Satār hāṇz,* Satār the boatman; *Satrām sarrāf,* Satrām the banker; *Rasul khār,* Rasul the blacksmith.

189. In the same way, the word for "city," "village," "island," "sea," etc., is used after the proper name, meaning "city of," etc., in English; as, *Amritsar shahr,* the city of Amritsar; *Makahom gām,* the village of Makahom; *Sōna lōṇk,* the island of Sōna (gold) in the Dal Lake, near Srinagar.

Case.

(1) *Nominative Case.*

190. The nominative case is used with intransitive verbs in all tenses, and with transitive verbs in the present, future, and past imperfect tenses; as, *Amritsar chhu ak bōdh shahr,* or *Amritsar chhu bōdh shahrā,* Amritsar is a large city; *Diarwōlⁱ chhė zulm karān garīban* (*gharīban*), The rich oppress the poor; *Bō dimạ,* I will give; *Suh os pakān,* He was going; *Suh os wuchān,* He was seeing; *Tim pakⁱ,* They went; *Tsạ osuk pōkmut,* Thou hadst gone.

191. When a clause or sentence forms the subject of a verb, it is regarded as its nominative, and the verb will be in the singular number, and in the case of an infinitive with a noun, the verb will agree with it in gender also; as, *Kẹṇh hechun prath dohạ chhu zarur*, It is necessary to learn something every day; *Köm karaṇⁱ chhè insānas kits jān!* How good is it for man to work!

192. The verbs *āsun*, to be; *sapanun*, to become; *banun*, to be made or become, etc., take the nominative case after them; as, *Suh chhu mahniu*, He is a man; *Tamis mahniv sund dil chhu sapanmut kaṇⁱ*, That man's heart has become stone; *Nechu bani mahniu*, The son will become a man; *Deg chhè teg* (proverb), The pot is a sword.

193. When the same nominative is common to two or more verbs, it is expressed before the first only; as, *Suh chhu khèwān, chèwān, tạ shongān*, He eats, drinks, and sleeps. If, however, emphasis is required, the noun or its representative pronoun may be expressed before each verb; as, *Sāhib chhu hospitāl gatshān, tạ suhī* (or *sāhib*) *chhu bīmāran hinz khismat karān*, The sahib goes to the hospital, and he (also) attends to the sick.

(2) *Accusative Case.*

194. No noun has any particular form for the accusative in Kashmīrī; it is the same as the nominative, but comes after the verb, as in English, whilst the nominative comes before the verb. A pronominal affix is also generally added to the verb to indicate the accusative; as, *Suh māri mahniu*, He will beat the man; *Mahniu māri suh*, The man will beat him. With the affix: *Suh mārin mahniu*, He will beat him, the man; *Mahniu mārin suh*, The man will beat him (he or it). In this example, as both the nominative and the accusative are third person singular, the accusative is only known by its position after the transitive verb. But when the

nominative and the accusative are not of the same person and number, the verb will always agree with its nominative and the pronominal affix with the accusative, and as the pronominal affixes are very generally used, there are thus generally two accusatives; as, *Bò māra mahniu*, I will beat, or kill, the man; but better with the pronominal affix, *Bò māran mahniu*, I will beat him, the man; so, *Bò mārak mahniv*, I will beat them, the men.

195. *Present tense.* *Bò chhus mārān mahniu*, I am beating the man; or better with the pronominal affix, *Bò chhusan mārān mahniu*, I am beating him, the man.

196. *Past tense.* After the past tense (not imperfect) of a transitive verb the accusative always agrees with the verb in number and gender; as, *Mēh mor hāput*, I killed a he-bear; *Mēh māri hāpatsa*, I killed she-bears; *Gurʾau mor hāput*, The horses killed a he-bear; *Timau os mormut tsur*, They had killed a thief.

(3) *Genitive Case.*

197. The genitive affixes, *-sund*, *-hund*, *-uk*, *-un*, and *-uv*, are all inflected and agree with the noun possessed in number and gender.

198. When the same noun governs two other nouns joined by the conjunction *tạ*, in the genitive case, the sign of the genitive is only placed after the second, though both nouns are inflected; as, *Buḍʾen tạ lokatʾen hanz khidmat gatshi nạ karani*, It is not proper to take (literally, to do) the service of the old and young.

199. When a noun in the genitive case governs another in the genitive, then the sign of the genitive in the first noun is inflected; as, *tsurasandis nechiviạnz kur*, the daughter of the son of the thief; *mahnivsandis gurisạnz lākam*, the bridle of the horse of the man (of the man's horse); *meziki takhtuk rang*, the colour of the wood of the table; *mezichi*

kitābihund jild, the cover of the book of the table; *Panani garuk hāk-wāk chhuī beyisandis pulāwas barābar*, The vegetable of thine own house is to thee equal to the pulau of another (person).

200. But when two nouns come together, both in the genitive case, with *sund* or *hund*, the one noun governing the other, the inflected sign of the genitive of the first noun is generally omitted, leaving the second noun with its inflected genitive sign; thus, instead of *tsurasandis nechivsaṇz kur*, we have *tsura nechivsaṇz kur*, the thief's son's daughter; so *sāhiba naukaranhund asbāb*, instead of *sāhibanhandⁱen naukaranhund asbāb*, the things of the sahib's servants. The sign of the genitive is sometimes omitted; as, *chhāna kīj*, for *chhānasaṇz kīj*, the carpenter's wooden peg; *hunis athi auṭ māndanāwun*, to knead flour with a dog's paw (proverb).

201. But when the governing word has *-uk* or *-ki*, the *-ki* of the preceding genitive is not omitted; as, *garki* (or *gharki*) *diwāruk chunạ*, the lime of the wall of the house; *garki diwāraki chunaki phaluk rang*, the colour of a piece of the lime of the wall of the house.

202. If the last noun is in the dative case, being governed by a preposition, then the sign of the genitive of the noun immediately preceding it has *s* added to the *-ki*; but if there are more genitives before this, they have the *-ki* only; as, *chunakis phalis pèṭh*, upon a piece of lime; *garki diwāraki chunakis phalis pèṭh*, upon a piece of the lime of the wall of the house; so, *sāhibasandi garki diwāraki chunakis phalis pèṭh*, upon a piece of the lime of the wall of the house of the sāhib.

203. The affix *-uk* is only used with inanimate objects, but there is no restriction as regards the objects possessed. *Yih shahrach sāwènⁱ khèyi tih khèyi gāmach gāw*, The lady of the city will eat this which the cow of the village will eat; *Āmanuk ṭòṭ*, a pony of Āman (a village); *Dobisund hun, nạ garuk tạ nạ gāthuk*, The washerman's dog is not of the (does

not belong to) house nor the g͟hāt; *Hārạch gogaj tạ Lārạch gunas chhi barābar*, A turnip of (the month) Hār and a gunas (snake) of (the district) Lār are equal.

204. The genitive affix *-un* is only used with proper nouns, but the noun possessed may be masculine, feminine, or neuter; as, *Mīrza Razāhun gāḍa-āra*, the fish necklace of Mīrza Razā; *Musa K͟hānun kastur*, Musa K͟hān's blackbird; *Miskīn S͟hāhun āstān*, the āstān (ziārat, or place of pilgrimage) of Miskīn Shāh. *Hyuh* may also govern the genitive in *-un*; as, *Namrūdun hyuh dam diwān* (proverb), He boasts (literally, gives breath) like Nimrod.

205. Though *-uk* and *-uv* may both be translated by "of," yet there is a difference in their meanings: *-uk* means "of," *i.e.* "in the possession of," or "for the use of;" *-uv* means "of," but "made of," and represents the English termination "-en." "A box of gold" in English may mean a box full of gold, or a box made of gold, *i.e.* a golden box. In Kashmīrī the first would be *sònuk sanduq*, a box of gold, *i.e.* containing or for the use of gold; but the latter, *sònuv sanduq*, a box of gold, *i.e.* a box made of gold—golden. *Tresh chènuk pöni*, drinking-water (*pīne ka pānī*); *behanạch jāī*, a place for sitting; *khènuk waqt*, time of eating.

206. Price or value is often put in the genitive case; as, *dahan rupīyan hund thān*, a thān (piece of cloth) of ten rupees (value); *trehan hatan rupīyan hund gur*, a horse of (the value of) three hundred rupees.

207. In the same way, age or time of life; as, *Yih shur chhu satan rètan hund*, This child is seven months old (This child is of seven months).

208. A genitive placed between duplicated nouns has an intensive force; as, *Tami niov garuk garai*, He took away the house altogether; *Shahruk shahrai gau ābād*, The whole city became peopled.

209. The genitive is used for the object of hope, feeling,

sentiment, etc. *Mè chhè tasandi yinach ummed*, I have hope of his coming; *Suh chhu Kodāyi* (*Khudāyi*) *sund mahabat thawān*, He loves God; *Mēh chhu chon bīm*, I fear him.

210. Ability and worthiness may be sometimes indicated by the genitive; as, *Yih gur chhu na kuni kāmihund*, This horse is of no use.

211. In definitions and explanations. *Gurun chhu aki kisamach göd*, The gurun is a kind of fish.

212. The genitive is sometimes governed by a noun, not expressed but understood. *Mion boz*, for *Mion hāl boz*, Hear my condition; *Miöni boz*, for *Miöni khat boz*, Hear my word.

213. When anything is represented as belonging to several persons, and their names occur in a series with the conjunction *ta* between the last two only, then the sign of the genitive is only used with the noun before and the noun after the *ta*; as, *Yih gara chhu Mohan Lāl, Rām Chand, Jawāhir Lālun, ta Benī Lālun*, This is the house of Mohan Lāl, Rām Chand, Jawāhir Lāl, and Beni Lāl.

(4) *Dative Case.*

214. The dative case denotes the recipient, and may generally be expressed in English by "to." After active verbs it points out that in which the object of action rests; and after the verbs *āsun*, *sapanun*, etc., it means "belonging to." *Mè diut kalam tas*, I gave a pen to him; *Be-hayāhas sharm* (*chhu*) *dur*, To the shameless shame is distant; *Hul kya kari sèdis?* What will the bent (man) do to the straight (one)?

215. The dative is very frequently used to denote "belonging to," both with nouns and pronouns, and also with pronominal affixes to verbs. *Batas tsèd, Musalmānas yad, ta Rāfizaas hud*, To the Hindu belongs endurance, to the Musalmān (Sunī) stomach, and to the Shī'a lamentation; *Chānis*

hākas chhu nạ pāk dinuk hājat, The necessity of cooking is not to your vegetable (It is not necessary to cook your vegetable); *hāpatas ai auṭ āsihe*, If there were flour to the bear (if the bear had flour); *Dazanas dod* (proverb), Pain belongs to burning; *Khudā chhu ṭhulas zu diwān* (proverb), God gives life to the egg; *Kya chhuī nāw?* What is your name? *Sas chhum basti. Salih chhum nāw*, I have pulse in my bag. Salih is my name; *Kāshīrī kahai gara* (proverb), Kashmīr has only eleven houses.

216. The dative is constantly used in connection with verbs denoting "giving," "speaking," "appearing," "coming," "happening," "going." *Sāni dohach tsot bakhsh az asi*, Give us this day our daily bread; *Ak mondiladan yit kòr tas sijda tạ dòpnas, ai Khudāwand, tsạ ai yatshak mė hakak ṣāf karit. Yasu'an dòpun*, A leper having come, worshipped Him, and said to Him, O Lord, if Thou wilt Thou art able to make me clean. Jesus said; *Dapahas ai ābas gatshun, gatshi khushkas; dapahas ai khushkas gatshun, gatshi ābas*, If I were to tell him to go to the water, he will go to the dry land; if I were to tell him to go to the dry land, he will go to the water; *Manani yiyi nạ panani, tạ hahadānas rėh?* (proverb), Its own flame (fire) will not come to the manan (small kāngri) and to the hahadān (large fireplace)? *i.e.* The manan has no fire, then how can it supply fire for the hahadān? *Mėh chhu m'alum*, It is evident to me, *i.e.* I know; *Tas peyi*, It will happen to him; *Panun panun garạ gatshiu*, Go each one to his own house; *Mė pėov shur bīmār*, My child happened to be ill.

217. The dative is sometimes used for price or value; as, *Mė hiut hatas rupīyas gur moli*, I bought a horse for one hundred rupees; *Mė kun garạ shīthan rupīyan*, I purchased a house for sixty rupees.

218. It is frequently used for time; as, *subhas*, in the morning; *shāmas*, in the evening; *rātas*, at night; *dohas*, by day. *Subhan, shāman*, etc., are also used. *Rātas wòninas*

Lail; paga dòpnas, "Sòh kya wātihe Majnunas?" At night he told him (of) Lail; on the morrow he said to him, "What will she be (arrive) to Majnun?" *Tam[i] wòn jawāl dit timan shāman chhiva tòh[i] wanān zi paga āsi hawa rut tikyazi āsmān chhu wuzul, tạ subhan chhiva wanān zi az kari wau,* And He answered them, and said, In the evening ye say that to-morrow the air will be fine, because the sky is red, and in the morning ye say that to-day will be rough.

219. The dative is often used where we should use the objective in English; as, *lusamatis lāyun,* to beat a tired (man); *Suh chhu mèh mārān,* He is killing me; *kharas khasit tạ buth path kun karit,* having mounted the donkey, and having turned the face backward, *i.e.* with the face towards the tail; *Mion mol chhu mè mahabat karān,* My father loves me; *Nechu mālis minnat karān,* The son beseeches his father; *Dachhun atha chhu chhalān khowaris, tạ khowur atha chhu chhalān dachinis* (proverb), The right hand washes the left, and the left hand washes the right; *Suh chhu timan nād diwān,* He is calling (to) them.

220. The object of any feeling or emotion is often put in the dative; as, *Mè chhu tasund mahabat,* I love him; *Tas chhu mion hasad,* I envy him; *Yim tohi neki karān timan tih kariu tòh[i] neki,* Do good to those who do good to you.

221. The dative with the verb *āsun,* followed by the infinitive used as a verbal noun, is sometimes used to express duty, propriety, or necessity; as, *Mèh asi gatshun,* I shall have to go; *Tsèh chhuī hechun,* You must learn; *Insānas chhu marun,* Man must die; *Nechivis chhu parun,* A boy should read.

222. The verbal noun in the dative (gerund) is used to express purpose; as, *Suh chhu kŏm karanas taiyār,* He is ready to work; *Bòh chhus prārān gatshanas,* I am expecting to go.

223. The dative is often used for salutations and good wishes; as, *Tòhih āsinavạ salāmati,* Peace (and safety) be to

you; *Timan āsin umr-darāz*, Long life be to them; *Tōh[i] kariu pānawāṇ[i] ak akis salām*, You amongst yourselves salute each other (one the other).

(5) *Case of the Agent.*

224. The case of the agent is only used with transitive verbs in the past tenses (not the imperfect), and generally where *ne* would be used in Hindustānī; the verb, or verb and past participle, then agree with the (what would be in English) objective in gender and number.

Thus from the transitive verb *mārun*, to kill or beat, we have the past indef. tense *mor*, and the past part. *mormut*; and these must agree with the object killed in gender and number; and in the past perfect tense, where the verb *āsun* is used with the participle, both the verb and participle must agree in gender and number with the object killed; and in the same way with the pluperfect tense.

Examples—

Tsuran mor hāput, A thief killed a he-bear; literally, A he-bear (was) killed by a thief.

Tsuran mör hāpats, A thief killed a she-bear; literally, A she-bear (was) killed by a thief.

Tsuran mör[i] hāpat[i], A thief killed he-bears; literally, He-bears (were) killed by a thief.

Tsuran māri hāpatsa, A thief killed she-bears; literally, She-bears (were) killed by a thief.

So with the past perfect tense—

Tsuran chhu mormut hāput, A thief has killed a he-bear; literally, A he-bear was killed by a thief.

Tsuran chhė mörmạts hāpats, A thief has killed a she-bear; literally, A she-bear was killed by a thief.

Tsuran chhi mör[i]mat[i] hāpat[i], A thief has killed he-bears; literally, He-bears were killed by a thief.

Tsuran chhè mārimatsa hapatsa, A thief has killed she-bears; literally, She-bears were killed by a thief.

So with the past pluperfect—

Tsuran māriov (or *māreyov*) *hāput*, A thief had killed a he-bear; literally, A he-bear had been killed by a thief.

Tsuran mārey hāpats, A thief had killed a she-bear; literally, A she-bear had been killed by a thief.

Tsuran mārey hāpati, A thief had killed he-bears; literally, He-bears had been killed by a thief.

Tsuran māreyī hāpatsa, A thief had killed she-bears; literally, She-bears had been killed by a thief.

Tsuran os mormut hāput, A thief had killed a he-bear, etc.

Tsuran ös mörmats hāpats, A thief had killed a she-bear, etc.

Tsuran ösi mörimati hāpati, A thief had killed he-bears, etc.

Tsuran āsa mārimatsa hāpatsa, A thief had killed she-bears, etc.

225. A peculiarity to be remembered with respect to the personal pronouns in the agentive case is that the second person singular always has the pronominal affix *-t* added to the verb, and the second person plural *-va*; the other personal pronouns may have their proper affixes added to the verb or not; they are generally added. We can say, *tami mor hāput*, or *tami morun hāput*; but we cannot say, *tse mor hāput*; it must be *tsò morut hāput*; so *tòhi chhuva mormut hāput*, and not *tòhi chhu mormut hāput*.

226. In Hindustānī the verb *bolnā* does not take *-ne* with the agent, but with *dapun* and *wanun* the agentive case must be used; as, *bāp bola*, the father said; *main bola hun*, I have said; but in Kashmīrī, *māli dòp*, or *māli wòn*; *mèh chhu dòpmut*, *mèh chhu wònmut*.

227. The agent may sometimes come after the verb, but there cannot well be any mistake made in recognizing it

with its own inflection. *Shur niov pāzan, tạ shistar khēyov gagaran* (proverb), The hawk took the child, and the rat ate the iron.

228. The agentive case, however, generally precedes the verb; as, *Bujī labiov kujī tal tsunṭ; ada gayi phōt hēt,* An old (woman) had found an apple under a tree, then she went (there) with a basket (having taken a basket).

229. It should be noticed that in the first declension the agentive case singular and the dative plural are the same, but they can be easily recognized by the context; as, *Tsuran mor hāput,* A thief killed a bear; *Tsuran chhu hāput,* The thieves have a bear.

(6) *Locative Case.*

230. The locative case denotes situation, the place in which or at which something is or is done; its form is the same as that of the dative, but it is accompanied by a preposition expressed or understood. The most common of such prepositions are *manz, manzbāg,* within, in the middle; *andar,* in; *nish,* beside, near; *pēṭh,* upon. *Shahras manz chhu lukh rozān,* People live in the city; *Bāgas* (*bāghas*) *manzbāg chhu kul,* There is a tree in the middle of the garden; *Mezas pēṭh chhu kalam,* There is a pen on the table; *Mēh nish chhu gur,* A horse is beside me; *nakha,* close to.

231. The preposition *nish* with a noun is sometimes used to denote possession; as, *Tōhi nish chhuā kalam?* Have you a pen? *Yemis mahnivis nish chhi guri,* This man has horses; *Tōhi nish chhuā mion wunṭh kinạ tasund gur?* Have you my camel or his horse?

(7) *Ablative Case.*

232. Motion from a place, or the source from which anything proceeds, is denoted by the ablative case, which is generally governed by the above prepositions with *-ạ* or *-ī*

added to them; thus, *manza*, from within; *andara*, from under or amongst; *nishī*, from beside; *pètha*, from upon. *Katī pètha āk?* Where hast thou come from? *Gāma pètha*, From the village; *Bò ās Dīwān Sāhibas nishī*, I came from the Dīwān Sāhib; *Yih nechu chhu yiwān bāga andara*, This lad is coming out of the garden; *Sāravöi jānwarau andara* (or *manza*) *chhu hòst bòd*, The elephant is the largest of (from amongst) all animals; *Dòda nishī chhè than[i] nerān*, Butter comes from milk; *Gurī nishī chhu gatshān paida bachi*, A colt is born from a mare.

233. The preposition is not always expressed. *Bòh ās shahra*, I came from the city; *Kāgaz chhu banān zach[i]au*, Paper is made from rags; *Dai ai diyī ta bara nyāsai* (proverb), If God will give, He will give to thee (cause thee to take) at the door.

234. The manner in which, and the means or instrument by which, anything is done is put in this case; as, *Yih mahniu chhu sāri tāqata söt[i] köm karān*, This man works with all his might; *Suh chhu panan pān pananī shamsherī söt[i] mārān*, He is killing himself with his own sword; *Yih chhu nāra söt[i] banān*, This is made with fire.

(8) *Vocative Case.*

235. The vocative is the case of address, or that form of the noun used in calling attention. It can generally be very easily recognized either by a preceding interjection or by its own termination. *Hā māli! hā maji!* (proverb), O father! O mother! *Ai sāni māli!* O our father! *Hakīmas ta hākimas nishi rachhtam Khudāyo!* (proverb), From the doctor and the ruler, O God, deliver me! *Kòkari handi batak thùlo, tsa kawa zānak "titī tī"?* (proverb), O duck's egg of (hatched by) a hen, when wilt thou know the hen's call (*titī tī*)? *Ai hāk, tsa kati āk?* O cabbage, where hast thou come from? *Putra, khar*

tsōl! O son, the ass ran away! *Neko, nek kar tạ bad labi pānai!* (proverb), O good (man), do good, and the bad (man) will receive his own (deserts)!

4. Adjectives.

236. Every adjective, or term used adjectively, must qualify a subject expressed or understood. The adjective, as in English, generally precedes the substantive it qualifies. If the adjective be one that is declined, it agrees with its substantive in gender and number; thus: *Ṛut nechu*, a good son; *rạts kur*, a good daughter; *rati nechiv*, good sons; *ratsa kori*, good daughters.

237. An adjective qualifying two or more nouns agrees generally with the one nearest to it; as, *Mol tạ kur chhè rạts*, The father and daughter are good; *Kur tạ mol chhu rut*, The daughter and father are good.

238. When an adjective qualifies a noun in the genitive case, the noun only takes the sign of the genitive, and the adjective is inflected; as, *badis mahniv sund nechu*, the big man's son; *badi sanduquk dasta*, the handle of the big box.

239. *Hawāva* and *moya* are used for liquids and things that cannot be said to have pieces, much as *thoṛa* in Hindustānī is used, only these always come after the noun, whilst *thoṛa* as an ordinary adjective precedes and agrees with its substantive in gender and number. Strictly speaking, *hawāva* is a noun, from *hawā*, air, and means "a whiff or puff of air," and so *ābạ hawāva* would be *ābạ sund hawāva*, a whiff of water, a little water.

In the same way, *hana* means literally "a piece of," and is thus applied to substances that can be divided into pieces, much like *chhoṭā* in Hindustānī, only, like *hawāva* and *moya*, always following an inflected substantive. *Mönai* is used with *hana moya* and *hawāva*; as, *mönai doda hana*, a very little milk; *mönai āba moya*, a very little water.

240. *Kėṇh* and *keṇtsa* are used with adjectives; as, *Yih kėṇh mȯdur chhu nạ*, This is not at all sweet; *Yih tsunt chhu keṇtsa tsȯk*, This apple is a little sour.

Comparison of Adjectives.

241. As has already been noticed, there are no regular suffixes or inflections to mark the degrees of comparison of adjectives. It will be sufficient here to give some examples of the way in which this difficulty is met in Kashmīrī. *Mion garạ chhu tahandi khȯta thȯd* (or *tsor thȯd*), My house is higher than his; *Bȯh chhus tahandi khȯta mihrbān* (or *tsor mihrbān*), I am kinder than he is; *Suh sanduq chhu yemi sanduqa khȯta tsor bȯḍ*, That box is much larger than this box; *Kus chhu madrasas manz sitha lȯkut nechu?* Which is the smallest boy in the school? (Who is the very small boy in the school?); *Miānis tabelas manz chhu yih gur sitha bȯḍ*, This horse is the biggest in my stable (In my stable this horse is very big); *Sārivai mājiau manzạ ös soi sitha mihrbān*, She was the very kindest of all mothers; *Suh chhu sārivai nechiviau manzạ rut*, He is the best of boys; *Suh nechu chhu panani bėni hindi khȯta kam gātul*, That boy is less clever than his sister.

5. Pronouns.

(1) *Personal Pronouns.*

242. There is no word of respect in Kashmīrī like *āp* in Hindustānī. When gentlemen converse together they always use the pronoun in the second person plural in addressing each other, as in English and Persian; when they speak to inferiors they often use the second person singular.

243. Persons of rank, in speaking of themselves, use the first person plural, and not the first person singular. This is much like the custom that prevails in India amongst those who speak Hindustānī.

244. The third person singular is always used in speaking of a person in his absence, no matter what his dignity may be. The plural is often used in Hindustānī. *Āj Dīwān Sāhib chhu yiwān, tą köm kari shahras andar*, To-day the Dīwān Sāhib is coming, and he will work in the city; *Kas sipāhas chhu pādshāh nād diwān?* What soldier is the king calling?

245. The accusative of *bòh* is *mèh*; and *tsèh* is sometimes used as the accusative of *tsą*. For "He is beating me," we can say, *Suh chhu mèh mārān*, or *Suh chhum mārān*, or *Suh chhum mārān mèh*; but we cannot say, *Suh chhu mārān bòh*, nor *Suh chhum mārān bòh*. For "He is beating thee," I find some pundits say, *Suh chhusat mārān tsą*; but others say, *Suh chhusai mārān tsèh.*

246. When a personal pronoun is accompanied by a qualifying noun in apposition, the sign of the genitive is used only after the noun, but the pronoun is in an oblique case; as, *mèh faqīri sund garą*, the house of me, the faqīr; so *tsèh faqīri sund garą; tas faqīri sund garą*, etc.

247. *Yih* and *suh* are often used as demonstrative pronouns; as, *yih gur*, this horse; *suh shur*, that child.

(2) *Reflexive and Possessive Pronouns.*

248. *Pāną*, self, is used with nouns or pronouns; as, *Pundit chhu pāna yih köm karān*, The pundit himself is doing this work; *Bò gos pāną*, I myself went.

249. *Pān*, body, self, and *panun pān*, own self, are also used for "self," and sometimes without a preceding noun or pronoun; as, *Luka hund katit nèthanun pān; Luka handi rachhit nèputra pān* (proverb), Himself naked, having spun (the wool) of (other) people; himself childless, having taken care of (the children) of (other) people; *Yih na bānas lāri tih lāriā pānas?* (proverb), This will not stick to the pot, and will it stick to one's self? *Jān kus chhu? Panun pān* (proverb), Who is good? My own self; *Khèwān pānas tą thèkān jąhānas*, He eats to himself and boasts to the world.

250. *Pānai* is the intensive form of *pānạ*; it is sometimes used in the sense of "alone;" as, *Bò gos pānạ*, I myself went; *Bò gos pānai*, I alone went; *Natsān tih pānai tạ wāyān tih pānai* (proverb), He himself alone dances, and he himself also plays; *Panun muhim chhu hāwān pānai wat*, One's own difficulty points out the way its own self.

251. *Pānawān[i]* is used for "amongst ourselves, yourselves, or themselves;" as, *Yih köm pānawān[i] kariu*, Do this work amongst yourselves; *Tikyāzi wati pakān ös[i] tim pānawān[i] bahạs karān zi asī andar kus chhu bòḍ*, For walking by the way they were disputing amongst themselves who is the greatest amongst us (literally, that who is great among us).

252. *Panun*, own, always refers in Kashmīrī to the nominative or agent of the sentence; as, *Mol chhu pananis nechivis paranāwān*, The father teaches his son; *Möj chhė panani kori paranāwān*, The mother teaches (literally, causes to read) her daughter; *Yih chhė mė panani kitāb*, This is my own book; *Tòh[i] chhiva pananis naukaras nād diwān?* Are you calling your servant?

253. *Panun* is sometimes repeated to denote separation; as, *Tim sāri luk chhi panun panun garạ gatshān*, All those people are going to their own (separate) houses (literally, house). If we simply said, *Tim sāri luk chhi panun garạ gatshān*, it would mean, "All those people are going to their own (one) house."

254. *Panun* is often used substantively, meaning "one's own relations, friends, or people;" as, *Suh chhu gatshān pananien nish*, He is going to his own—people or friends; *Panun ai māri shihalis trāwi, parud ai māri tạ māritoi gatshi* (proverb), If one's own (relation, etc.) should kill (me, etc.), he will place in the shade (the grave); but if a stranger should kill (me), immediately after killing he will go away; *Panan[i]au chhu nạ paighambar monmut* (proverb), His own (people) have not obeyed (their) prophet.

255. The possessive pronouns agree with their substantives in number, gender, and case. *Chon munga trak son sun ak* (proverb), Thy trak (about twelve pounds) of mung (is) his one meal; *Chānis dahānas gulāb* (proverb), Rose-water (or, a rose) to his mouth; *Suh mahniu chhuā tihund dost?* Is that man their friend? *Yih chhuā tuhund wunth? Nạ, yih chhu nạ son*, Is this your camel? No, this is not ours; *Yih chheā tasanz kur? Sȯh chhė tasanz kur*, Is this his daughter? She is his daughter; *Yih chhė nạ tihanz kitāb*, This is not their book.

(3) *Demonstrative Pronouns.*

256. Demonstrative pronouns agree with their substantives in number, gender, and case. *Yih hun chhu khėwān*, This dog is eating; *Hȯh zanānạ chhė gatshān*, That woman is going away; *Yiman mahniv'en hund gur tsȯl*, These men's horse ran away; *Yath gāmas nạ gatshun āsi tami gāmuk nāwoi hėun kya chhu?* (proverb), Why inquire the name of that village to which (you) have not to go? (literally, To the village there may not be to go, of that village why take the name?).

257. The substantive is often omitted. *Yih chhu bich yut rachhihan tut diyi toph* (proverb), this is a scorpion, as many as nourish it, so many it will sting; *Mėh nish nạ chhu yih tạ nạ suh*, I have neither this nor that; *Suh kus chhu? Suh chhu mion dost*, Who is that? He is my friend; *Gur zanānạ, shamsher, yim trenawai chhi be-wafā*, A horse, a woman, a sword, these three are unfaithful.

(4) *Relative Pronouns.*

258. The relative pronouns *yus* (masc.), *yȯsạ* (fem.), and *yih* (neut.) answer to the English relatives "who," "which," or "what;" and they are followed by *suh*, *sȯh*, and *tih*, as correlatives. When the relative is accompanied by a sub-

stantive, it agrees with the substantive in number, gender, and case; but, unlike the order observed in English sentences, the relative in Kashmīrī is usually found at the beginning of a sentence. *Yus gatshi suh wāti*, (He) who will go, he will arrive; *Yōsa kur panani māji māni sōh bani jān möj*, The daughter who obeys (or, will obey) her own mother, she will become a good mother; *Yih mol chhu karān, tih chhu nechu hèchhān*, What the father does, that the son learns; *Yusoi khèyi ser suī gatshi ser* (proverb), He who shall eat a ser (seer, two pounds), he will be satisfied; *Yus yas zāni sui tas māni* (proverb), Whom he knows, him he will obey (literally, Who whom he may know, he him will obey); *Yiman gabar, timan na bata; yiman bata, timan na gabar* (proverb), Those who have children, they have no food; those who have food, they have no children; *Yih tsèh chhuī wandas tih chhu mèh chandas* (proverb), That which thou hast in the heart, that I have in the pocket; *Yimavoi mor imām, timavoi kôr sama* (proverb), Those very persons who killed the imām, they made the lamentation; *Yih malla wani tih gatshi karun; yih malla kari tih gatshi na karun*, That which the mullā may say, that (we) ought to do; that which the mullā may do, that (we) ought not to do.

259. Though the relative agrees with its substantive, expressed or understood, in number, gender, and case, yet the relative and correlative may be of different cases, though always of the same number and gender. *Yemⁱ kôr 'ār suh gāw khwār*, He who did a meanness, he became mean; *Yusoi rōchhum tasi nish rachhtam Khudāyo* (proverb), He who was taken care of by me, O God, take care of me from him; *Yemⁱ wuchh naris ta dalis suh gāw khwār* (proverb), He who looked to the sleeve and border, he became mean.

260. *Akā*, *kanh*, and *kantsa* may be joined to *yus* and *yosa*, which then denote "whoever;" *kènh* can be used with *yih*, which will then denote "whatever." The correlatives re-

ceive no additions. *Yus akā guṅah chhu karān suh chhu panun nuqṣān tsāṇḍān*, Whoever sins seeks his own injury; *Tahanzi māji dòp naukaran yih kèṇh suh waniva tih kariu*, His mother said to the servants, Whatever He says to you, that do.

261. The intensive forms are *yusoi*, *yiī*, *suī*, etc. *Nunan dopus*, "*Yusoi gòl suī gòl*," The salt said to it, "That which melted, that melted;" *Won[i] gāw suī yus pānis bozi hisāb* (proverb), He indeed is a shopkeeper who will understand the account of water; *Yusoi ròchhum yiman athan, suī yiwān netharan kathan* (proverb), He whom I cherished with these hands, even he is coming with words about marriage.

(5) *Interrogative Pronouns.*

262. The interrogative *kus*, who, is inflected, and agrees with its substantive, expressed or understood, in number, gender, and case. *Huh mahnuv kus chhu?* Who is that man? *Sòh zanānạ kòsa chhèh?* Who is that woman? *Yih nechu kòhund chhu?* Whose child is this? *Kahand[i] nechiv mör[i] pādshāhan?* Whose children did the king slay? *Kam[i]uk hājat chhuī?* What have you need of?

263. *Kaṇh* for masculine and feminine, and *kèṇh* for neuter nouns are used as interrogatives with the interrogative form of the verb. *Kaṇh chhuā garas andar?* Is there any one in the house? *Yath sanduqas andar kèṇh chhuā?* Is there anything in this box?

(6) *Other Pronouns.*

264. *Kaṇh*, any masculine and feminine singular, and *kèṇh*, some, are thus used: *Mèh chhè nạ kaṇh kitāb*, I have not any book (I have no book); *Mèh chhè nạ kèṇh kitāba*, I have not any books (I have no books); *Timan os nạ kaṇh chīz*, They had not anything; *Timan os nạ kèṇh*, They had nothing; *Khudāwand chhu nạ panani w'ada bāpat susti karān yitih pöṭh*

kenh chhi susti ganzarān balki suh chhu tuhandi khōtira sabar karān zi kōnsi hanz halākat chhu na yatshān, The Lord is not slack concerning His promise, as some (men) count slackness; but is long-suffering to you-ward, not willing that any should perish; *Ta yeli tōhi du'ā mangana khātira chhiva istāda sapanān tōhi ai kōnsi pēth kēnh shikāyata āsiva tas kariu m'uāf,* And when ye are standing to pray, if ye have some complaint against any one, forgive him; *Kanh aka chhu na farzandas zānān magar mol,* No one knoweth the Son, but the Father; *Kanh naukar chhu na don āghan hanz khidmat karit hēkān,* No servant is able to serve two masters; *Muhtājan di kēnh,* Give something to the poor; *Tami waqta ösi kēnh zani hāzir,* At that time some persons were present; *Tau pata wōn tahandiau kēntsau tsātau pānawōni yih kya chhuh?* Then some of His disciples said amongst themselves, What is this?

265. *Beyāk,* another; *kustām,* some one. *Tikyāzi agar suh yus yiwān chhu beyis Yasu'a sanz manādi karihe yēmi sanz na asih kar, yā beyāk ruh labihiu yus na tōhi lōbwa, yā beyāk injīl yōsa na mejmats ösiva ta tihund bardāsht karun os jān,* For if he that cometh preacheth another Jesus, whom we did not preach, or if ye receive a different spirit, which ye did not receive, or a different gospel, which ye did not accept, to bear with him was well; *Lekin Yasu'an dōpus kamitām lōg mēh atha,* But Jesus said, Some one touched me; *Fakhara söti ma kariu kanh köm lekin halīm dili söti zānion ak beyāk panani khōta behtar,* Do nothing with boasting, but with lowliness of mind, let each esteem the other better than himself.

266. *Har,* each, every, is Persian, and is sometimes used by those who know that language for the Kashmīrī word *prat,* which has the same meaning. They are both joined to *kanh, kēnh, aka,* etc.; as, *Har rang-i-musībat chhu ak diwānagī* (proverb), Every kind of misfortune is a madness; *Prat kanh yus muhabat chhu thawān suh chhu Khudāyas nishi paida sapunmut,* Every one who loveth is begotten of God; *Prat kanh rats*

bakhshish tạ prat kaṇh kāmil in'ām chhu az bālā, Every single good gift, and every single perfect gift, is from above; *Prat kaṇh kul chhu panani mewa söt[i] parzanāwana yiwān*, Every single tree is known by its fruit; *Pas prat aka diyi Khudāyas panun panun ḥisāb*, Therefore every one shall give his own account to God.

267. Most of the compound pronouns are formed by adding *kaṇh, kèṇh, aka*, and *tām* to the personal relative and interrogative pronouns; as, *Pas ai ādmi yus aka āsi*, Therefore, O man, whosoever he may be; *Yeli nạ tòh[i] begāna sandis mālas andar rudiva diyānatdār kus aka diyiva tòhi tih yih tahund āsi?* When ye have not been faithful in another's property, who will give you that which is yours? *Yih kèṇh tòh[i] mion nāw hèt mālis nish mạngiu suh diyiva tòhi*, Whatever ye shall ask the Father in My Name, He will give it you.

268. *Ak akis söt[i]*, one with another, or one another; *Thaviu ak akis söt[i] mahabbat*, Love one another. *Ak akis pèṭh*, one upon another, one another; *Ak akis pèṭh ma kariu grāva*, Murmur not one against another. *Ak aksund*, one of another; *Sörai 'azuv rozan pānawön[i] ak ak sandi hamdard*, Let all the members remain amongst themselves in sympathy one with another.

6. Verbs: Use and Application of the Tenses.

(1) *Active Voice.*

269. As has been already remarked, the verbs in Kashmīrī are generally very regular.

(*a*) *Indicative Mood.*

270. *Present tense.* There is only the present continuous tense of verbs in Kashmīrī (except the verb *āsun*) formed by the active or present participle with the auxiliary verb "to be." We can say, *bò chhus*, I am; *su chhu*, he is; but the only

way of saying "I do," "he does," is *bô chhus karān*, I am doing; *su chhu karān*, he is doing. The auxiliary agrees with its nominative in number and gender, the participle is not inflected; the auxiliary also takes the pronominal affixes, not the participle. *Saruf chhu pakān hôl hôl tạ wāj tal wātit syud* (proverb), The snake goes crookedly (crooked crooked), and having reached its hole (it is then) straight; *Shīn ḍeshit yih gagur kari tih chhuk rupīyi ḍeshit karān* (proverb), What the rat, having seen the snow, will do, that thou art doing having seen rupis; *Bô chhusava tôhi ak nav hukm diwān zi ak akis söt[i] kariu muhabbat*, A new commandment I give unto you, That ye love one another.

271. The auxiliary verb is sometimes not expressed, but is always understood; thus: *Sarrāf ganzarān diyār, tạ atrāf rāwarān dôh* (proverb), The banker counts the money, and the spendthrift wastes the day; *Sarafa sạnzạ sat zêwa* (proverb), A snake's seven tongues; *Gur jān, sum jān, yāl jān, chāl jān, kadam nai* (proverb), The horse (is) good, hoof good, mane good, appearance good, but (there is) no step; *Hun[i] worān tạ kārawānạ pakān* (proverb), The dogs bark, and the caravan goes on; *Huni-wushkạ yur nạ wawān tur bowān* (proverb), Dog-barley (tares) where (we) do not sow there they grow.

272. It must be observed that *chhus* may mean "I am," or *chhu tas*, to him, he has; so *chhuī* may be the intensive form of *chhu*, or it may mean *chhu tsê*, to thee, thou hast. The right meaning will be easily gathered from the context; thus: *Bô chhus köm karān*, I am working; *Ak wonān wagavī beyāk pilanāwān chhus pêts* (proverb), One weaves the mat, and another holds out to him the reed; *Khoja chhu khushī karān ki nechu chhum gāṭul; nechu chhus pāma diwān ki moloi chhum be-aql* (proverb), The khoja rejoices that he has a wise son (to me is a wise son), the son gives him reproach because he (the son) has a foolish father (that the father indeed to me is without understanding); *Tsê chhuī nạ gur*, Thou hast

not a horse; *Chhāna thukas chhuī ras taiyār* (proverb), To the hammering of the carpenter the soup is ready; *Chhānas tạ bāzigaras tạ shahsawāras chhui audui umr* (proverb), To the carpenter, and the tumbler, and the horse-breaker there is indeed only half a life, or, The carpenter, etc., have only half a life.

273. The ordinary way of expressing "I have," "he has," "they have," etc., in Kashmīrī is by putting what is the nominative case in English in the dative case, and making the verb agree with the noun possessed in number and gender; thus: "I have a book," is, in Kashmīrī, "To me is a book," *Mė chhė kitāb. Tas chhė kėṇh kitābạ*, He has some books; *Timan chhi nạ gurⁱ*, They have no horses; *Tôhi chhuvā ak bad shakl wunṭh?* Have you an ugly camel? *Timan chhu hāput*, They have a bear; *Munanⁱėn hunⁱėn shaposh ta mė nạ kalaposh tih* (proverb), Muna's dogs have a quilt, but I have not even a skull-cap. In the same way we speak of the past and future: *Mė os gur*, I had a horse; *Tas āsi kalam*, He will have a pen.

274. We can also say, *Brāri nish chhu gagur* for "The cat has a rat;" *Sôn gur os na timan nish?* Had they not our horse? *Tôhi nish chhuā kalam?* Have you a pen? *Mion wunṭh chhuā akis mahnivis nish?* Has a man my camel?

275. The indefinite past tense of *gatshun* is often used for the present tense, meaning "it became," and so "is." *Rasa rust bata gāw ṭhasa rust chhān* (proverb), Rice without soup is a carpenter without noise; *Ak tạ ak gāw kah* (proverb), One and one make eleven; *Waqtuk kār gāw takhtuk pādshāh* (proverb), The work of the time is the king of the throne; *Shur gāw bror; "Wula, wula," karus tạ yiyi* (proverb), A little child is a cat; repeat, "Come, come," and it will come.

276. Two nouns joined by the copulative conjunction *tạ* frequently take the verb in the singular; as, *Mol tạ möj chhė garas andar*, The father and mother are (is) in the house;

Āw tạ gâw (or *jāw*) *chhus barābar* (proverb), Come and gone (*i.e.* finding and losing) are (is) alike to him; *Bukhāri gayi nāsūr-i-khāna* (proverb), The fireplace is the ulcer of the house; *Kur gayi lori rust piyāda* (proverb), A daughter is a runner without a stick.

277. *Future tense.* The future tense is sometimes used for the present. *Yus yuth kari suh tyuth suri; yus yuth wavi suh tyuth loni* (proverb), As he does, so he receives; as he sows, so he reaps; *Yus yas zāni suī tas māni* (proverb), He obeys him whom he knows; *Kār-i-Khudā zāni Khudā* (proverb), God knows the work of God; *Yus akā khèyi tạ chèyi tạ kanṣi diyi, suh chhu jān tasandi khòta yus ani tạ jama' kari* (proverb), Any one who eats and drinks and gives to another is good compared with him who brings and hoards; *Pish kari gunāh wagavis chob, wuchhtau lukau tamāsha!* (proverb), The flea sins, the mat is beaten; behold, O people, the sight!

278. The intensive future is formed by adding *i* to the simple future. *Zānai nạ qaum, nạ krām, nạ nām* (proverb), I certainly will not know your nation, or class, or name.

279. *Future interrogative. Gur dapiā ki mion dod chhu tsòk?* (proverb), Will the milkman say that my milk is sour? *Yus nạ gaba phaṭi suh dapiā "Baba"?* (proverb), He who is not born (to me), will he say, "Father"? *Pāni rust dāni khasiā zi nāni rust shur khasi?* (proverb), Will rice rise up without water, that the child should grow up without a grandmother?

(For the future used as subjunctive, see Subjunctive Mood.)

280. *Past tenses.* It is only necessary to remark on those past tenses formed by means of a participle and the auxiliary verb "to be," as the imperfect, perfect, and pluperfect (second form), that, when a pronominal affix is added, it is always joined to the auxiliary verb, not to the participle; and that the active participle undergoes no change for number,

gender, or person, whilst the perfect participle always agrees in number and gender with its noun, which in the case of an intransitive verb is the nominative, and in the case of a transitive verb what would in English be the objective. *Suh os mė lāyān*, He was beating me; *Tim ösi mė lāyān*, They were beating me; *Mė chhimava tòhi dunyaha nishi tsārit juda karimati*, I, having chosen you, have separated you from the world.

281. The past indefinite of intransitive verbs always agrees with its nominative in number, gender, and person. There are two forms of conjugation which differ slightly from each other. Some verbs of this tense are conjugated like *pòkus* and *sapanus*, and others like *doryos* and *gos*. In the case of the second kind the pluperfect is only a lengthened form, as *doreyos*, *doreyov*, etc.; but in the first kind the consonant preceding the personal terminations often undergoes a change, as *pòkus*, *pòk*, *pachos*, *pachiov*, or *pachios* (*pachyos*), *pachyov*, *pacheyov*. The longer form appears to throw the time further back than the shorter: *Doryos*, I ran, *doreyos*, I had run; *pachos*, I had gone, *pacheyos*, I had gone before that. *Phul phòṭ ta da'wā kya?* (proverb), The line (or, connection) broke, then what (is) the complaint? *Kati, bāi, āk?* Whence, brother, camest thou? *Sirini ās*, I came from Sirin.

282. The past indefinite and pluperfect (first form) of transitive verbs always agree with (what would be in English) their objectives in number and gender. *Hash gayi ta noshi kòr ārām* (proverb), The mother-in-law went (died), and the daughter-in-law had (made) peace; *Yemi kòr ār su gāw khwār* (proverb), He who did the shame, he became shameful; *Pīriau maryov dānd mėh kya rāvyov zi bòh wanihe kānsi?* (proverb), The pīrs had killed an ox: what had I lost that I should tell any one? *Bujī labiov kujī tal tsunt; ada gayi phòt hėt* (proverb), An old (woman) had found an apple under a tree, afterwards she went (there) having taken a basket;

Lekin yih sapun yuth suh kalām yus tihandis sharī'atas andar likhit chhu zi timau kar mėh söti be-sabab dushmani pur sapani, But this came to pass that the word which in their Law is written, that they hated Me without a cause, might be fulfilled.

(For the use of the pluperfect as a subjunctive, see Subjunctive Mood.)

(*b*) *Imperative Mood.*

283. There is nothing requiring particular mention in the use of the simple imperative; but special attention should be paid to (1) the use of the respectful imperative; (2) the use of the pronominal affixes with the imperative; and (3) the termination *-zi* added to the imperative, which gives it a future signification. *Mėh ti ditam yenāma,* Be pleased to give me also a reward; *Wuchhtau kyạ pyau husnas wāv; rānṭasi kòruk Shāh Māl nāw* (proverb), Behold, what misfortune has happened to beauty! they gave to the ugly woman the name Shāh Māl; *Shīna pėtau! Bāyi yitau!* (proverb), Fall, O snow! Come, O brother! *Tạ tami wòn tas yih zi Khudāwand yus chon Khudā chhu panani sāri dili söti tạ panani sāri 'aqli söti kar tas muhabbat . . . tạ pananis hamsayas kar yuthai muhabbat yuth pānas chhuk karān,* And He said to him this, that the Lord who is thy God, love thou with all thy heart, and with all thy mind . . . and love thy neighbour as thou dost love thyself; *Hakīmas tạ hākimas nishi rachhtam Khudāyo!* (proverb), O God, deliver me from the doctor and the ruler! "*Pīra, wantam masalā!*" *dòpnas,* "*akī gom tasallā*" (proverb), "O pīr, tell me an example!" he said to him; "one was enough for me;" *Poshākan chhu wònmut,* "*Tāh kartam shāh karat*" (proverb), The garment has said, "Fold me up (take care of me), and I will make thee a king;" *Khudā ma karin!* God forbid! (May God not do it!); *Yeli su yiyi mė karzi khabar,* When he comes, tell me (When he will

come, give me word); *Kur dizi nạ Ishibari* (proverb), Give not a daughter to an Ishibari; *Yih hakīmas dizi tih kona dizi bīmāras?* (proverb), That which thou wilt give to the doctor, why not give to the sick?

(For the use of the verb with the termination *-zi* as a subjunctive, see Subjunctive Mood.)

(c) *Subjunctive Mood.*

284. The present tense of the subjunctive mood is the same as the future; thus: *Bŏ chhus āmut yuth tim zindagī laban tạ zyāda ḥaṣil karan,* I am come that they may have life, and that they may obtain more (life); *Tŏhi chhiva nạ yatshān zi me nish yiyiu yuth zindagī labiu,* You do not desire to come to Me that you may have life; *Nādān ai zāni zi nādān chhus, ada chhu nạ nādān* (proverb), The ignorant man, if he knows that he is ignorant, then he is not ignorant; *Panani kŏkạr nai bad āsi tạ luka hundi gari kyāzi trāwi ṭhul?* (proverb), Your own hen, if she were not bad, then why does she lay eggs in the house of other people? *Khor ai āsi bilkul ṣāf toti āsanas hat phephara* (proverb), If a person with a bad head (suffering from impetigo capitis) be perfectly clean, yet there will be a hundred pimples left.

285. The verb with the termination *-zi* is used sometimes with *ai*, if, as a subjunctive; as, *Dachh ai khĕzi tạ āpaimān; kachh ai khĕzi tạ zyur* (proverb), If thou shouldst eat grapes, then āpaimān; if thou shouldst eat grass, then zyur; *Mangawun ai thavizin ṭanga-wani andar tati tih kari mangamang* (proverb), If thou shouldst place a beggar in a pear-grove, even there he will beg; *Hāri ai wunṭh kunun āsi tạ hār nai āsi tạ karizis kya?* (proverb), If a camel should be sold for a cowrie, and thou hast not a cowrie, then what canst thou do? *Pitur ai dizin kala kin dānas zangau sŏti phutarāwi rupeyi bāna* (proverb), If thou shouldst thrust an uncle head fore-

most into the fireplace, with his legs he will break a rupee's worth of cooking-pots; *Pitur ai dizin penⁱ tati tih tsaṭi yenⁱ* (proverb), If thou shouldst give an uncle the pen[i] (cleaning-brush), then also he will cut the yen[i] (warp).

286. The past indefinite is used to express a wish or a condition; as, *Kāshke suh āsihe hāzir!* Would that he were present! *Gara, wandai gara sāsā! gara, neraha na za!* (proverb), O house (home), I offer thee a thousand houses! home, would I might never leave thee! *Kāshke tòh[i] karihiu saltanat tạ ạs tih karahau tòhi söt[i] saltanat!* Would that ye did reign, that we also might reign with you! *Su ai panani gari āsihe tạ tahanz mòj āsihe seṭha khush*, If he had been at home, then his mother would have been very pleased; *Mèh ai banduq āsihe tạ bò lāyaha zarur tas*, If I had had a gun, I certainly should have shot him; *Tim ai bīmār āsahan tạ tahanz beni āsihe seṭha ghamgīn*, If they were (or, had been) ill, then their sister would be very sorry; *Hāpatas ai auṭ āsihe tạ su karihe nạ tsochi?* (proverb), If a bear had flour, would he not make bread? *Yih shakhs nai Khudāya sandi ṭarafa āsihe kènh hèkihe nạ karit*, This Man, if He were not from God, could do nothing; *Tạ tạm[i] Farīsīyan, yem[i] tas sāl os kòrmut, yih wuchhit wònun dilas andar, zi yih ai nabi āsihe tạ zānihe zi yih zanāna, yòsa amis chhè atha lāgān, kòsa chhè tạ kitsh chhè, tikyāzi gunahgār chhè*, And that Pharisee who had given the invitation, having seen this, said in his heart, that if this (Person) were a prophet, then He would know that this woman who touches Him who she is, and what kind (of woman) she is, for she is a sinner; *Ai Khudāwand, tsạ ai yati āsahak mion boi marihe nạ*, O Lord, if Thou hadst been here, my brother had not died.

287. *Pluperfect.* *Bò nai āsaha āmut tạ timan dapaha nạ tihund gunāh āsihe nạ, lekin won[i] chhu nạ timan nish tihandi gunāhuk 'uzar*, If I had not come and spoken to them, they had not had sin, but now they have no excuse for their sin.

(*d*) *Participles.*

288. The indefinite active participle in *-ān* corresponds to the active participle in English ending in "-ing;" as, *karān*, doing; *pakān*, going; and is used with the auxiliary verb in the same way as the participle in English. *Bò chhus karān*, I am doing; *Bò āsa karān*, I shall be doing; *Bọ osus karān*, I was doing, etc. *Pāṇsa nishi chhu pāṇsa phaṭān* (proverb), A paisā is bursting from a paisā.

289. The active participle is also used as a continuative and statistical verb; as, *Parān, parān par gāi khāli* (proverb), Reading, reading (by constant reading), the feathers have become empty; *Magar Petrus rod ṭhas ṭhas karān*, But Peter remained knocking; *Su nechu chhu yiwān giwān giwān*, That boy comes singing.

290. The perfect or past participle is inflected to agree with its noun in number and gender; with intransitive verbs the noun with which the perfect participle agrees is the nominative, and with transitive verbs the (what would be in English) objective. *Tikyāzi tuhạndⁱ tsāṭ ösⁱ shahras andar gāmatⁱ*, For His disciples were gone into the city; *Wuchiu gar chhė yiwān balki āmats chhė zi tòhⁱ sapaniu paraganda prat akah pananⁱen nish*, Behold, the hour cometh, yea, is come, that ye shall be scattered every man to his own; *Ai Māli gar chhė wātsmats*, Father, the hour is come; *Tòhi chhiva rāstbāzas pėṭh hukm kòrmut qatl chhus kòrmut tạ su chhuva nạ muqābala karān*, You have condemned the righteous (man), you have killed him, and he doth not resist you; *Zi tòhi sāranai hund os mushtāq tạ yemi khöṭira zi tòhi ösⁱva tuhanzi bīmāri hund ḥāl bozmut ghamgīn os*, For he longed after you all, and because that you had heard of his state of sickness, he was very sorry; *Mė chhu chon nāw timan insānan pėṭh ẓāhir kòrmut yim tsė dunyaha andarạ ditit mė; tim ösⁱ chönⁱ, tạ tim*

chhit tsė mė ditimati; tạ timau chhė chānis kalāmas pēṭh 'amal karmats, I have made known Thy Name to those men whom Thou gavest me out of the world; they were Thine, and Thou hast given them to Me; and they have kept Thy Word.

(e) *Conjunctive and Adverbial Participles.*

291. The conjunctive participle is indeclinable. It is used to connect the different members of a sentence having the same nominative, and in this way obviates the use of the copulative conjunction. It therefore takes the place of the verb and a conjunction. It implies the completion of the action denoted by it prior to another action denoted by a subsequent verb. It may be rendered in English by "having done, said," etc., or by "and" with the verb. *Bar dit khar natsān* (proverb), Having shut the door, the ass dances, or The ass shuts the door and dances; *Wāv wuchhit gatshi nāv trāwaṇi* (proverb), It is proper, having (first) observed the wind, to loose the boat; *Shungit bāng dapaṇi* (proverb), Having gone to sleep to call the bāng (the Muhammadān call to prayers); *Tāki yih kėṇh mion nāw hėt mālis mangiu su diyiva tòhi,* That whatsoever, having taken My Name, ye shall ask of the Father, He may give it you; *Shamsher kaḍit yotshun zi panun pān māri,* Having drawn (his) sword, he was about (he desired) to kill himself.

292. The form of the conjunctive participle is always used with the verb *hėkun,* to be able; as, *Bò chhusava yim miöni dost chhiva wanān zi timan nish mạ khotsiu yim badanas chhi qatl karān tạ tau pata chhi nạ beyi kėṇh karit hėkān,* I say unto you who are My friends, Fear not them who kill the body, and after that are able to do nothing more; *Kus chhu zi amis haiwānas söti hėki jang karit?* Who can make war with this beast? *Pas timau trov zāl tạ gaḍan ḳandi kasrata*

söṭi hiukuk nạ zāl khārit, Therefore they cast the net, and with the multitude of fishes they were not able to draw the net.

293. It is sometimes used where we might have expected the active participle; as, *Yuth nạ be-khabar pöṭh yit tòhi shungit wuchhiva,* Lest coming (having come) unexpectedly, he should find you sleeping; *Tạ beyi yit wuchhin tim shungit,* And again having come, He found them sleeping; *Yeli ạsi shungit ösi,* When we were sleeping; *Mē wani yimạ katha tòhi söṭi āsit tòhi,* These things I spoke unto you, being with you.

294. It is sometimes used where we might have expected the past participle; as, *Yeli Herodīsan su ḥāẓir karun yotsh tami röts os Patrus doyau hāṅkalau söṭi gaṇḍit don sipāhan manzbāg shungit,* When Herod desired to bring him forth, that same night, Peter, bound with two chains, was sleeping between two soldiers; *Tạ t'alīm dit farmovun timan kya likhit chhu nạ zi miānis garas yiyi sārien qauman handi 'ibādatuk gara wanana?* And He taught and said unto them, Is it not written, My house shall be called a house of prayer for (of) all nations? *Tạ kitāb mutsarit laban sò jāi yati likhit os,* And having opened the book, He found the place where it was written; *Zi tuhạndi nāw chhi āsmānas peṭh likhit,* For your names are written in heaven.

295. This form is sometimes used with a second verb, which agrees with the noun, but which often serves only to intensify the meaning of the conjunctive participle; sometimes the two verbs together form a compound with a distinct meaning. *Pas chöni dachan achh ai tsè khunt khèā-wanuk bā'iṣ āsi tạ kaḍit tshunun su trāwit dur,* Therefore if thy right eye cause thee to stumble, pluck it out and cast it from thee; *Tạ su peau wasit,* And it fell; *Tau pata chhu dapān, pananis garas andar gatsha pot phīrit,* Then he says, I will return to my own house; *Bò chhus chon t'arīf karān zi*

tsė thawit yim chīz dānahan tạ gāṭilan nish khaṭit lekin shur'en pėṭh karit zāhir, I thank Thee that Thou didst hide these things from the wise and prudent, and didst reveal them unto babes. (The second person of the past tense of the verb with the pronominal affix *-t* must be distinguished from the conjunctive participle.)

(*f*) *The Infinitive.*

296. The infinitive signifies the action denoted by the verb without any direct reference to the agent or the time. It is really a verbal noun, and as such is constantly used in Kashmīrī.

297. It is governed by another noun or pronoun in the possessive case; as, *Ạm' kòr haikal nāpāk karanuk qaṣd*, He endeavoured to defile the temple; *Zanāni hund asun chhui mardas manzimyor* (proverb), A woman's laugh is a go-between to the man; *Zanāna chhė prasani wizi tauba karān* (proverb), A woman at the time of travail repents; *Zanāni hund yāwun gaṇḍun tạ chhāwun; wethi hund yāwun wubalāwun; wiri hund yāwun ṭak dāwun; marda sund yāwun dan* (proverb), The woman's adornment is putting on jewels and dress; the river's adornment is casting up waves; the willow's adornment is cutting off the branches; the man's adornment is wealth; *Chānis hākas chhu na pāk dinuk hājat* (proverb), Your (thy) cabbage has no need of cooking.

298. It may be used as a nominative to a verb, or governed by a preposition. *Koli tshunun chhu āsān, tạ khārun mushkil* (proverb), To throw into the stream is easy, and to take out difficult; *Yih bata chhu nạ khėnas lāiq*, This food is not fit to eat; *Yih karun chhu nạ tòhi munāsib*, It is not proper for you to do this; *Khudāwand Yesu' sanzạ katha yād thawani zarur zi tam' dòp diun chhu hėna khòta mubārak*, It is necessary

to remember the words of the Lord Jesus that He said, It is more blessed to give than to take.

299. The inflected infinitive is frequently used to denote the object of an action. *Bô chhus zamīnas pêṭh nār dini āmut*, I am come to cast fire upon the earth; *Tôhi chhiva gumān karān zi bô chhus zamīnas pêṭh ṣulḥ karani āmut?* Do you suppose that I am come to make peace on the earth?

300. The infinitive is sometimes used with the verb "to be," like the Latin gerund, to denote necessity or obligation; as, *Ākhir chhu aki dôha marun tạ sāroi kêṇh chhu trāwit gatshān*, At last one must die (*moriendum est*) and leave everything.

301. In the case of nominals, the infinitive always agrees with its noun in gender; as, *Lub karun chhu gunāh*, It is sin to covet; *Lekin neki tạ sakhāwat karaṇi ma mashrāwiu*, But to do good and to distribute forget not.

(2) *Passive Voice.*

302. The passive voice of the verb in Kashmīrī is very regular; it will be sufficient, therefore, to give some examples of its use. *Yuth guris yiyi ratana wag tiuth paki barābar* (proverb), As a horse's (to a horse) bridle is held, so he will go exactly; *Tạ sardār kāhinan tạ faqīhan hindi atha tula seṭha taklīf tạ mārana yima*, And from the chief priests and scribes (at the hand of) I shall suffer much, and I shall be killed; *Agar kaṇh shamshera söti chhu mārān ẓarur chhu zi suh yiyi shamshera sötoi mārana*, If any one kills with the sword, with the sword must he be killed; *Yim nạ timau āfatau söti mārana ösi āmati*, Who had not been killed by these plagues; *Tạ mê boz timan hund shumār yiman pêṭh muhr karana āyi*, And I heard the number of those who were sealed (upon whom a seal was made).

7. Adverbs.

303. There is no definite position invariably observed for adverbs in a sentence; generally they are placed near the words they qualify; as, *Wāra wāra pakiu*, Go slowly; *Saruf chhu pakān hul hul*, The snake goes crookedly.

304. The word *ma*, not, used with the imperative instead of *na̤*, is always used before the verb; as, *Tsa̤ ma kar khun*, Thou shalt not kill; *Tsa̤ ma kar zinā*, Thou shalt not commit adultery; *Yih ma kariu gumān, zi bò ās tauret ya nabiyan ha̤nz kitāb zāy'a karani*, Suppose not that I came to destroy the Law or the book of the prophets.

305. The negative *na̤* is generally used after the verb, almost invariably after the verb "to be;" as, *Bò ās na̤ zāy'a kara̤ni*, I came not to destroy; *Bò chhus na̤ tas nād diwān*, I do not call him; *Mion gur chhu na̤ yèti*, My horse is not here. The *nā* in an interrogative may come before the verb; as, *Yih nā chhè tiha̤nz kitāb?* Is not this their book? *Na̤ tihanz chhè na̤*, No; it is not theirs.

306. A repetition of words may alter the meaning or intensify it; *ak ak*, one by one, or, every one; *dòha dòha*, day by day; *ta̤kān ta̤kān*, quickly; *wāra wāra*, slowly.

8. Prepositions.

307. Prepositions are used with the nouns they govern, and always after them, not sometimes before and sometimes after, as in Hindustā̤nī. *Padis tal tungul* (proverb), A live coal under the foot; *Pāni rust dāni khasiā zi nāni rust shur khasi?* (proverb), Will rice grow up without water, that a child should grow up without a grandmother? *Chāni shara nishi rachnam Khudāi!* May God preserve me from thy wickedness!

308. The Persian and Arabic prepositions are used more

by the Musalmāns than by the Hindus, and amongst the Musalmāns those who know and speak Persian use them most frequently. The Persian preposition *barāe*, with the word *Khudā* in the phrase, *Barāe Khudā*, For God's sake, is constantly heard everywhere.

309. It would seem that all the prepositions that govern the genitive case are derived from nouns. *Nakhạ*, near, is from *nakh*, the shoulder, and means literally "by the shoulder;" *nakhạ tal*, close by, means literally "under the shoulder;" *nāwạ*, for, for the sake of, is from *nāw*, a name, and means literally "for the name of;" so, *khōtirạ* from *khāṭir*; *sababạ* from *sabab*; *tarafạ* from *taraf*, etc.

310. The same preposition may govern two or more cases; but generally it has then a different meaning in each case. *Sōtⁱ*, meaning "by means of," may take the genitive or ablative case; and, meaning "with," "alongside," the locative case; as, *Suh au bayabānas andar Shaitānạ sandi sōtⁱ āzmāwanạ tạ jangalkin jānwaran sōtⁱ os rozān*, He was tempted in the wilderness by Satan, and was staying with wild beasts.

311. The preposition *nish* is often used for *nishi*, but generally the case of the noun will show whether it means "to," or "near," or "from;" as, *Suh chhu gatshān shahras nish*, He is going to, or near, the city; but, *Su chhu gatshān shahrạ nish*, or better *nishi*, He is going from the city.

312. Proper nouns are not inflected with *nish*, but they take the *ạ* with *nishi*; as, *Suh chhu rozān Sopūr nish ya Shāhbād nish*, He lives near Sopūr, or Shāhbād; but, *Suh chhu yiwān yā Sopūrạ nishi yā Shāhbādạ nishi*, He is coming either from Sopūr or from Shāhbād.

9. Conjunctions.

313. The conjunction *ti*, or *tih*, can generally be easily distinguished from the pronoun *tih*. *Yas chhu tas yiyi dina tạ yas, nạ chhu tas yiyi ti tih hina yih tas chhu*, To him who hath

to him shall be given, and to him who hath not from him shall be also taken away that which he hath.

314. The following conjunctions are worthy of notice: *Ki na*, or; *Chhalana mal chhuā atsān ki na nerān?* (proverb), Does filth come or go with washing? *Yā . . . na ta*, either . . . or; *Yā pur na ta dur* (proverb), Either altogether or away; *Yā tsalun na ta tsālun* (proverb), Either flee or endure. *Na . . . ta na*, neither . . . nor; *Dobi sund hun, na garuk tą na gāthuk* (proverb), The washerman's dog belongs neither to the house nor to the ghāt. *Ti . . . ti*, also . . . also, or, whether . . . or; *Dog dit ti bāraw, dog het ti bāraw* (proverb), Whether he has given a blow or received a blow, he cries. *Ti na . . . ti na*, neither . . . nor; *Khoja, tsa ti yik na, ta bôh ti samakhai na za!* (proverb), O khoja, neither wilt thou come (to me), nor shall I meet thee evermore!

10. Interjections.

315. Kashmīrīs are particular about the interjections they use. Equals are addressed as "brother" or "sister," *hatabā* or *hatabin*; or as "sir," *hatasą*, the *-są* representing either the masc. *sāhib* or the fem. *sāhiba*.

316. *Haz* or *hazrat* is always used by Muhammadāns in addressing Muhammadān religious teachers and leaders, and often other Muhammadān persons of position as well; *shāh* is not so commonly used as *hazrat*, though it is used to Muhammadān officials.

11. Persian in Kashmīrī.

317. Persian having been used in Kashmīr for about three hundred years, and during most of that time as the court language and the tongue of the rulers, and being the language now generally used in official correspondence by

both Hindus and Muhammadāns, it would naturally be expected that many Persian and Arabic words, and even Persian phrases, should be found in modern Kashmīrī, especially as spoken by Muhammadāns. The following extracts will illustrate this :—

Be-kār chhu bīmār (proverb), The man without work is ill.

Be-kār chhu wakīl-i-har darbār (proverb), An idle man is the wakīl of every darbār.

Bukchi halāl tạ hār harām (proverb), The bundle lawful and the cowrie unlawful.

Bukhāri gayi nāsur-i-khāna (proverb), The fireplace is the cancer of the house.

"*Dāshtam, dāshtam,*" *chhu na bakār ;* "*dāram, dāram,*" *chhu bakār* (proverb), "I had, I had," is not necessary ; "I have, I have," is necessary.

Gari manz chhu garyāl, dam ghanīmat ast (proverb), At the hour the striker, breath is gain.

Gur, zanāna, tạ shamsher, yim trenawai chhi be-wafā (proverb), A horse, a woman, and a sword,—these very three are faithless.

Hakīmas tạ hākimas nishi rachhtam Khudāyo ! (proverb), Preserve me, O God, from the doctor and the ruler !

Halālas hisāb tạ harāmas azāb (proverb), Reckoning for the lawful and punishment for the unlawful.

Hukm-i-hākim o hakīm chhu marg-i-mafājāt (proverb), The command of the ruler and the doctor are (is) sudden death.

'Illat gali tạ 'ādat gali nạ (proverb), Sickness will depart, and habit will not depart.

'Ilmas 'amal (proverb), To knowledge action (is necessary).

'Izzatich hār tạ be-'izzatich khār chhė barābar (proverb), The cowrie of honour and the kharwār of dishonour are equal.

Jawānas nạ rozgār, lŏkatis mŏj maranⁱ tạ budis āshan maranⁱ ;

yim trenawai katha chhė sakht musībat (proverb), No livelihood for the young man, a dying mother for the little one, and a dying wife for the old one,—these three things are a terrible misfortune.

Jawān tạ jahān (proverb), Youth and the world.

Kalam-zan, shamsher-zan, kushti-zan chhi be-aqlas nish barābar (proverb), The writer, the soldier, (and) the wrestler are alike to the ignorant (man).

Kār-i-Khudā zāni Khudā (proverb), God knows (will know) the work of God.

Na "khair" tạ na "barakat" (proverb), Neither "good" nor "a blessing."

Nekan chhu Khudā-i-khush (proverb), God is pleased with the good.

Neknām chhė bekh-i-daulat (proverb), A good name is the root of wealth.

Neko, nek kar tạ bad labi pānai! (proverb), O good (man), do good, and the wicked will find his own (deserts)!

Namāz chhė farz, tạ luṭ chhu karz (proverb), Prayer is a duty, and plunder is a debt.

Niyatas mujib diyi tas Khudāi (proverb), God will give him according to his motive.

Pīr nạ bȯḍ; yaqīn bȯḍ (proverb), The pīr [saint] (is) not great; credulity (is) great.

Roghan o zāfarān az Pāmpūr, sāg az Lėtapūr, brinj az Nipūr, barra az Nandapūr, paṭṭu o māhī az Sopūr, moṇg az Krālapūr, ārad az Khāmpūr, shīr az Shādipūr, angur az Repūr (a common saying), Ghī and saffron from Pāmpūr, vegetables from Lėtapūr, rice from Nipūr, lamb from Nandapūr, cloth and fish from Sopūr, dal from Krālapūr, flour from Khāmpūr, milk from Shādipūr, grapes from Repūr.

Safar chhu qāfir (proverb), The journey is an infidel.

Sakhai diyi bār bār tạ bakhail diyi yak bār (proverb), The generous man will give time (after) time, and the miser will give one time.

Sharahas sharmoi kya! (proverb), What shame is there in the law!

Syud sāda chhu shāhzāda, A simple Syud (descendant of Muhammad) is a prince.

Yak tan tạ du kas (proverb), One body and two person.

Yā zuraw na tạ burāw (proverb), Either suffer or go.

Zān chhė jahān (proverb), Acquaintance is the world.

Zān na tạ pachhān na, tạ "khāla jī salām," Neither known nor recognized, and "Peace, Sir Uncle."

"*Zorạ, zorạ," nashi zu, tạ "Wāra, wāra," nashi koh* (proverb), "Quickly, quickly," wears away life, and "slowly, slowly," wears away a mountain.

CHAPTER X.

SENTENCES—ENGLISH AND KASHMĪRĪ.

318. What is it? *Kya chhu?*

What is this? *Yih kya chhu?*

Who is it? *Kus chhu?*

Is there any one there? *Tati chhuā kaṇh?*

There is no one, *Kaṇh chhu na.*

It is I, *Bòh chhus.*

Is it he? *Suh chhuā?*

Yes; it is he, *Ova; suī chhu.*

Is that a man? *Suh chhuā mahiniu?*

No; it is a bear, *Na; suh chhu hāput.*

Who is calling him? *Tas kus chhu nād diwān?*

Has he a horse? *Tas chhuā gur?*

What! has he not a horse? *Kya! tas chhu nạ gur?*

He had a horse, *Tas os gur.*

They had a horse, *Timan os gur.*

Have you not a pen? *Tòhi chhuva nạ kalam?*

Who has your dog? *Tuhund hun kas nish chhu?*

My dog was with your boy, *Mion hun os tuhand nechivi nish.*

He is a villager, *Su chhu gāmuk mahiniu.*

What are you doing? *Tòhi kya chhivā karān?*

Are you calling me? *Tòhi chhivā mė nād diwān?*

I do not call you, *Bò chhus nạ tòhi nād diwān.*

Whom do you call? *Tòhi kas chhivā nād diwān?*

I am calling him, *Bò chhus tas nād diwān.*

He is calling me, *Su chhu mė nād diwān.*

He is eating some bread, *Su chhu tsòchi hana khėwān.*

Does that man read the books that you read? *Suh mahniu chhuā tima kitāba parān yima tòhi chhiva parān?*

Why does he not read good books as I do? *Suh kona chhu miōni pöṭh ratsa kitāba parān?*

Why do not these men do their work well? *Yim mahnivi kona panaṇi köm wāra karān?*

Because they are always quarrelling with each other, *Tikya zi tim chhi hamesha ak akis söti jang karān.*

That boy always does what his father tells him, *Suh nechu chhu hamesha tih karān yih tasund mol tas chhu wanān.*

He says that it is very hot, *Suh chhu wanān zi sėṭha garm chhu.*

Where do you go every day? *Tòhi kòt chhiva prath dòha gatshān?*

Is that gun your own? *Tòhi chhuva suh banduq panun?*

I have several guns of my own, *Mē chhi panaṇi kėṇh banduq.*

He is talking with me, *Suh chhu mė söti katha karān.*

What is he saying to you? *Suh kya chhuva tòhi wanān?*

He tells me to come every day, *Suh chhu mė wanān zi prath dòha yun.*

He does what I tell him, *Yih bòh tas chhus wanān tī chhu karān.*

As long as your brother was here, all were well, *Yotāmat tuhund boi yeti os totāmat ös[i] sārī wāra.*

I have more than he, *Mè chhu tahandi khòta ziyāda.*

Is your brother at home? *Tuhund boi chhuā panani gari?*

No; he is far from home, *Na; suh chhu gara nishi dur.*

Is that book interesting? *Sòh kitāb chheā dilchasp?*

How far is the post-office from here? *Dāk-gara kota chhu yeti pètha dur?*

That book is on your table, *Sòh kitāb chhè tuhandis mezas pèth.*

He writes better than his brother, *Suh chhu pananis böi sandi khòta rut lekhän.*

This is impossible, *Yih chhu nā mumkin.*

319. Blessed are the poor in spirit: for theirs is the kingdom of heaven, *Mubārak chhi tim yim dilakin gharīb chhi: tikya zi āsmānach pādshāhat chhè timanai hinz.*

Blessed are they that mourn: for they shall be comforted, *Mubārak chhi tim yim ghamgīn chhi: tikya zi tasalli laban.*

Blessed are the meek: for they shall inherit the earth, *Mubārak chhi tim yim halīm chhi: tikya zi zamīnak[i] wāris sapanan.*

Blessed are they that hunger and thirst after righteousness: for they shall be filled, *Mubārak chhi tim yim rāstbāzi hand[i] bochhihat[i] ta treshihat[i] chhi: tikyazi āsuda sapanan.*

Blessed are the merciful: for they shall obtain mercy, *Mubārak chhi tim yim rahm-dil chhi: tikya zī timan pèth yiyi rahm karana.*

Blessed are the pure in heart: for they shall see God, *Mubārak chhi tim yim rahm-dil chhi: tikya zi Khudāyas wuchhan.*

Blessed are the peacemakers: for they shall be called sons of God, *Mubārak chhi tim yim sulh-karawan[i] chhi: tikya zi Khudāya sand[i] farzand yiyak wanana.*

Blessed are they who are persecuted for righteousness' sake: for theirs is the kingdom of heaven, *Mubārak chhi tim yim rāstbāzī hindi sababa taklīf chhu dina yiwān: tikya zi āsmanach pādshāhat chhė timanai hanz.*

Blessed are ye when men shall reproach you, and persecute you, and say all manner of evil against you falsely, for My sake, *Mubārak chhiva tōhi yeli miāni khōtira pāma, ta taklīf dinava, ta prat tarhach yachh katha apazi sōti tuhandis haqas andar wanan.*

Rejoice, and be exceeding glad: for great is your reward in heaven: for so persecuted they the prophets which were before you, *Shādmānī, ta khūshī kariu: tikya zi āsmānas pėth chhu tuhund ajr bōd: tikya zi yim paighambar tōhi bonth ōsi timan dituk yithai pōth taklīf.*

320. Our Father, which art in heaven, Hallowed be Thy Name. Thy kingdom come. Thy will be done in earth, as it is in heaven. Give us this day our daily bread. And forgive us our trespasses, as we forgive them that trespass against us. And lead us not into temptation; but deliver us from evil: for Thine is the kingdom, the power, and the glory, for ever and ever. Amen. *Ai sāni māli, yus āsmānas pėth chhu, Chon nāw sapanin pāk. Chōni pādshāhat yiyin. Chōni marzī yitha pōth āsmānas pėth chhė zamīnas pėth ti sapanin. Sāni dōhach tsōt bakhsh az asi. Ta sōni qarz kar asi m'uāf, yuth asi ti pananien qarzdāran chhi m'uāf karān. Ta asi ma an āzmāishi andar; Balki badas nishi rachh: tikya zi pādshāhat, ta qudrat, ta jalāl, chhu hamesha chhonai. Āmīn.*